DAILY SUMMER ACTIVITIES

BETWEEN GRADES 2 AND 3

Writing: Jo Ellen Moore
Content Editing: Marilyn Evans
Copy Editing: Cathy Harber
Art Direction: Cheryl Puckett
Cover Design: Liliana Potigian
Illustration: Jo Larsen
Design/Production: Cheryl Puckett

EMC 1029

Evan-Moor
EDUCATIONAL PUBLISHERS
Helping Children Learn since 1979

Visit
teaching-standards.com
to view a correlation
of this book.
This is a free service.

**Correlated to State and
Common Core State Standards**

**Congratulations on your purchase of some of the
finest teaching materials in the world.**

For information about other Evan-Moor products, call 1-800-777-4362,
fax 1-800-777-4332, or visit our Web site, www.evan-moor.com.
Entire contents © 2005 EVAN-MOOR CORP.
18 Lower Ragsdale Drive, Monterey, CA 93940-5746. Printed in USA.

CPSIA: Hess Print Solutions, 3765 Sunnybrook Road, Brimfield, OH 44240 [03/2013]

Contents

Skills

Skills	Week									
	1	2	3	4	5	6	7	8	9	10
Reading Comprehension										
Nonfiction	●	●	●	●	●	●	●	●	●	●
Fiction	●	●	●	●	●	●	●	●	●	●
Following Directions	●	●	●	●	●	●	●	●	●	●
Sequencing Events	●		●				●	●		
Who, What, When, Where, Why	●	●	●	●	●	●	●	●	●	●
Real/Make-Believe			●							
Inference		●	●	●	●	●	●	●	●	
Make Connections	●	●	●	●	●	●	●	●	●	●
Grammar/Usage/Mechanics										
Phonics		●	●	●	●			●		
Spelling	●	●	●	●	●	●	●	●	●	●
Alphabetical Order	●					●				
Contractions			●	●			●		●	●
Possessives		●	●		●	●	●			
Plurals	●						●	●		
Parts of Speech		●		●		●	●		●	●
Double Negatives	●				●	●		●		●
Vowels and Consonants	●	●	●	●		●		●		
Subject/Verb Agreement	●	●	●	●				●	●	
Abbreviations				●			●	●		
Capitalization	●	●	●	●	●	●	●	●		●
Punctuation	●	●	●	●	●	●	●	●	●	●
Syllabification					●		●			
Quotation Marks					●					
Analogies							●			
Vocabulary Development										
Rhyming Words		●						●	●	
Synonyms/Antonyms			●	●						●
Homophones	●				●	●	●			
Homographs			●							
Comparatives/Superlatives	●									
Compound Words		●								

Skills	Week 1	2	3	4	5	6	7	8	9	10
Writing										
Write a Sentence	•	•	•	•	•	•	•	•	•	•
Write a Paragraph			•		•					
Write a Story	•			•		•	•	•	•	•
Write a List		•		•					•	
Letter Writing	•									•
Handwriting										
Copy a Model/Practice Formations	•	•	•	•	•	•	•	•	•	•
Math										
Sequencing	•					•	•		•	
Read Number Words	•		•	•						
Word Problems	•	•	•	•	•	•	•	•	•	•
Greater Than/Less Than/Equal to		•						•		
Tell Time	•	•		•		•				•
Shapes		•				•		•	•	•
Money	•	•			•	•			•	•
Counting			•	•		•	•		•	•
Place Value			•	•	•					
Addition	•	•	•	•		•	•		•	•
Subtraction	•	•	•	•		•	•		•	•
Column Addition/Subtraction	•	•	•			•	•		•	•
Borrowing				•	•	•	•		•	•
Carrying				•	•	•	•		•	•
Multiplication					•		•	•	•	•
Graphs and Grids				•				•	•	•
Ordinals			•							
Fractions						•	•	•		
Measurement				•	•		•			
Geography										
Map-Reading Skills	•	•	•	•	•	•	•	•	•	•
Globes	•	•	•							
Compass Rose/Directions			•		•	•	•			
Legends								•	•	
Thinking Skills										
Riddles/Problem Solving	•	•	•	•	•	•	•	•	•	•

About This Book

What's in It

Ten Weekly Sections

Each section contains half-page and full-page activities that help children learn reading, writing, math, geography, spelling, grammar, and critical-thinking skills.

Each week, your child will work on the following:

Reading	▶ comprehension activities that include fiction and nonfiction topics
Spell It!	▶ an activity to practice the week's spelling words
Write It Right	▶ an editing activity to correct errors in spelling, grammar, and punctuation
Handwriting	▶ a writing activity to practice penmanship skills
Language Bytes	▶ activities that practice language skills such as abbreviations, parts of speech, and plurals
Math Time	▶ activities that practice math skills such as computation, measurement, and fractions
In My Own Words	▶ creative-writing exercises
Geography	▶ a map activity that tests basic geography concepts
Problem Solving	▶ a critical-thinking activity
What Happened Today?	▶ a place to record a memorable moment from the week, and a reading log to record the number of minutes spent reading each day

How to Use It

The short practice lessons in *Daily Summer Activities* prepare your child for the coming school year by making sure that he or she remembers all of the skills and concepts learned in second grade. After completing the activities in this book, your child will feel more confident as he or she begins the new school year. You can help your child by following the suggestions below.

> Provide Time and Space

Make sure that your child has a quiet place for completing the activities. The practice session should be short and positive. Consider your child's personality and other activities as you decide how and where to schedule daily practice periods.

> Encourage and Support

Your response is important to your child's feelings of success. Keep your remarks positive and recognize the effort your child has made. Work through challenging activities and correct mistakes together.

> Check in Each Week

Use the weekly record sheet to talk about the most memorable moments and learning experiences of the week and to discuss the books your child is reading.

> Be a Model Reader

The most important thing you can do is to make sure your child sees you reading. Read books, magazines, and newspapers. Visit libraries and bookstores. Point out interesting signs, maps, and advertisements wherever you go. Even though your child is an independent reader, you can still share the reading experience by discussing what you read every day.

> Go on Learning Excursions

Learning takes place everywhere and through many experiences. Build learning power over the summer by:

- visiting a zoo, local museum, or historic site. Use a guidebook or search online to find points of interest in your area.

- collecting art materials and working together to create a collage, mobile, or scrapbook.

- planning a calendar of summer events. Check off each event as you complete it.

- planting a garden. If you are short on space, plant in containers.

- creating a movie of your child's favorite story. Write a simple script and make basic costumes and props, and recruit friends and family members to be actors. Practice until everyone is comfortable before shooting the video.

Spell It! This list contains all of the weekly spelling words practiced in the book.

A

about
are
awake

B

bean
because
bench
black
bow

C

cake
check
clean
coat
cone
could
cute

D

down

E

egg
eight

F

find
first
fix
float
flower
friend
frown
funny

G

gave
girl
goat

H

happy
helped
her
house
hurt

J

jam
jumped
just

L

letter

M

man
many
most

N

no

P

paint
play
pull
push

R

rain
read
rose
round

S

saying
seen
sharp
she
should
shout
show
silly
skipping
sleep
slow
something
spot
start
stayed
stone
stopped
sweet
swimming

T

thank
this
throwing
time
today
toe
treat
turn

U

use

W

wait
wanted
wash
washing
water
week
went
were
when
who
with
would

Color a  for each page finished.

Parent's Initials

Monday   _____

Tuesday   _____

Wednesday   _____

Thursday   _____

Friday   _____

Spelling Words

jam	spot
egg	just
man	went
fix	black

What Happened Today? Write about one thing you did each day.

Monday _____

_____

Tuesday _____

_____

Wednesday _____

_____

Thursday _____

_____

Friday _____

_____

Keeping Track Color a book for every 10 minutes you read.

Monday	Tuesday	Wednesday	Thursday	Friday

My favorite book this week was

_____

I liked it because _____

_____

_____

My Pet Hen

Toby found a fluffy brown chick. He loved the little chick and took good care of her. "I'll call you Henny," said Toby.

Henny grew into a large red hen. Toby and his father built her a coop in the backyard. She had a place to roost at night, plenty of water, and good food. But Henny wanted to be with Toby. She would get out of the coop and go looking for him.

Every day, Toby heard someone call his name. "Toby! Get this chicken out of my kitchen!" or "Toby! Get your hen out of my car!"

One day, Father said to Toby, "I think Henny is lonesome. She needs to be with other chickens." They took Henny to Uncle Jay's farm to live with his chickens. It made Toby sad to leave Henny at the farm, but it made Henny happy to be with other chickens.

1. How did Toby get his chick?

   Toby got his chicken from a chicken farm.

2. How did Toby take care of Henny?

   Toby took care of her by feeding her and giving her water.

3. Why did people keep calling Toby?

   people cept calling toby because it was evlywere his parents were.

4. Why did Toby and Father take Henny to the farm?

   Toby and father took him to the farm because they thought she was lonly.

1. kan you come two my party

Can
_____

2. dont you have no cookies

any
_____

3. there is a lot of mouses in the shed

mouse
_____

MATH TIME   Add and subtract.

5 + 5	8 + 3	9 – 5	4 + 7	10 – 3	8 – 4	7 + 7	14 – 7	11 – 6	6 + 7
10	11	4	11	7	4	14	7	5	13

5 + 6	13 – 8	8 + 8	11 – 9	9 + 2	16 – 8	6 + 6	15 – 6	13 – 5	5 + 7
11	5	16	2	11		12	9	8	12

5 + 8	18 – 9	12 – 4	6 + 9	17 – 9	9 + 9	10 + 7	3 + 7	12 – 9	8 + 6
13	9	8	15	8	18	17	10	3	14

©2005 by Evan-Moor Corp. • Daily Summer Activities 2-3 • EMC 1029

Spell It!

Fill in the missing vowels.

| a e i o u |

j__a__m   sp__o__t   __e__gg   m__a__n

f__o__x   j__u__st   bl__a__ck   w__e__nt

Write sentences using the spelling words that have a short a.

1. I just brushed my teeth.

2. I spot a bunny.

3. I found an egg on my loun.

Write each letter using your best handwriting.

a b c d e f g h i j k l m
n o p q r s t u v w x y z

abcdefghijklmnopqrstuvwxyz

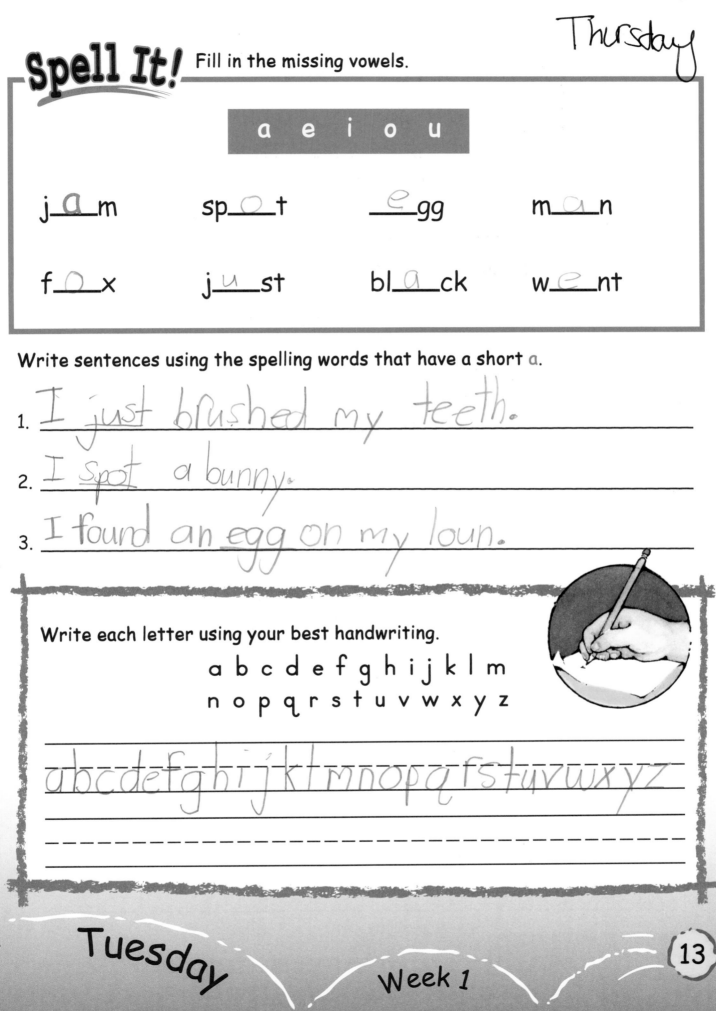

How do you spell more than one?

cat / **cats**   dish / **dishes**   man / **men**

1. boat _boats_
2. chair _chairs_
3. bench _benches_
4. goose _gooses_
5. balloon _balloons_

6. peach _peaches_
7. woman _woman_
8. dish _dishes_
9. jacket _jacketes_
10. wish _wishes_

MATH TIME

Write the numbers in each line in order.

69	70	66	71	68	72	67	73
_66_	_67_	_68_	_69_	_70_	_71_	_72_	_7_

70	90	100	80	60	110	50	120

58	64	52	50	62	54	56	60

205	235	210	220	225	230	215	240

237	561	729	386	175	663	480	893

©2005 by Evan-Moor Corp. • Daily Summer Activities 2-3 • EMC 1029

Chickens

Hens lay eggs. Some eggs are gathered as food for people. Some eggs are left in the hen's nest to hatch.

The hen sits on her eggs to keep them warm. She tucks the eggs under her body and turns them over with her beak.

Inside the eggs, chicks are growing. After about twenty days the chicks peck their way out of the eggs. When they hatch, chicks are small and covered with fluffy feathers. The baby chickens grow quickly. Before very long, they will grow into hens or roosters.

Number the pictures in order.

Name the chickens.

chicks   hen   rooster

rooster   hen   Chicks

Wednesday

Week 1

Language Bytes

Add the capital letters as you copy the address.

mrs. anna morgan — _Mrs. Anna Morgan_

16 maple avenue — _16 Maple Avenue_

lima, ohio 45802 — _Lima ohio 45802_

Write your address here.

Madeline claire long
your name

_15981_ _oakhurst lane_
street

fishers _indana_ _46040_
city   state   zip code

MATH TIME

Find the answers.

1. Louie saw 14 blackbirds sitting on a fence. Then 9 flew away. How many blackbirds are still sitting on the fence? __5__ blackbirds

2. Kai took 16 gumdrops. He gave half of the gumdrops to his friend. How many did he have left? __6__ gumdrops

3. Sam and Jim picked 12 baskets of berries together. If Sam picked 7 of the baskets, how many did Jim pick? __5__ baskets of berries

4. Tammy fixed a picnic lunch. She packed one sandwich, two cookies, and three carrot sticks for each person. How many things did she pack if six people went on the picnic?

__1__ sandwiches __2__ cookies __3__ carrot sticks

16

Week 1

Wednesday

©2005 by Evan-Moor Corp. • Daily Summer Activities 2-3 • EMC 1029

Ge🌐graphy

Draw a line from each riddle to the picture that shows the answer.
Write in the name of each picture to complete the sentences.

I am a model of the Earth.
I show where land and water
are located. I am round like
the Earth.

I am a ___map___.

I am a picture of the Earth.
I show where land and water
are located. I am flat.

I am a ___globe___.

Write a Story

I would like to have a pet ___dog someday I would___
___name it scruffles. I would take it___
___for walks, and feed it, and I would___
___give it a cunfy bed.___
_____.

Thursday   Week 1   17

MATH TIME

7, 9, 16

7 + 9 = 16

9 + 7 = 16

16 − 9 = 7

16 − 7 = 9

9, 8, 17

9 + 8 = 17

8 + 9 = 17

17 − 8 = 9

17 − 9 = 8

6, 7, 13

6 + 7 = 13

7 + 6 = 13

13 − 7 = 6

13 − 6 = 7

8, 4, 12

8 + 4 = 12

4 + 8 = 12

12 − 4 = 8

12 − 8 = 4

Write each list in alphabetical order.

A B C   a b c d e f g h i j k l m n o p q r s t u v w x y z   X Y Z

orange	1.	kiwi
pear	2.	orange
kiwi	3.	pear

goldfish	1.	beagle
parrot	2.	goldfish
beagle	3.	parrot

book	1.	bat
bike	2.	bike
bat	3.	book

wet	1.	warm
warm	2.	wet
wool	3.	wool

Week 1

Thursday

©2005 by Evan-Moor Corp. • Daily Summer Activities 2-3 • EMC 1029

Language Bytes

Circle the missing words.

1. Who on the team can run the __fastest__?

    fast   faster   ~~fastest~~

2. Sugar is __sweeter__ than salt.

    sweet   ~~sweeter~~   sweetest

3. Is Mother as __old__ as Father?

    ~~old~~   older   oldest

MATH TIME

What time is it?

_3_ o'clock
3:00

half past _2_
2:30

_5_ o'clock
5:00

6:30
half past _6_
6:30

11:00
_11_ o'clock
11:00

10:30
half past _10_
10:30

Connect the dots.
Start at 100.

t w e l v e f x
e i g h t l o s
n i n e m e u i
t h r e e v r x
f i v e t e n e
t w o z o n e y
r u n s e v e n

Find these numbers in the word search.

one	five	nine
two	six	ten
three	seven	eleven
four	eight	twelve

©2005 by Evan-Moor Corp. • Daily Summer Activities 2-3 • EMC 1029

Color a ⭐ for each page finished.

Parent's Initials

Monday	⭐ ⭐	_____
Tuesday	⭐ ⭐	_____
Wednesday	⭐ ⭐	_____
Thursday	⭐ ⭐	_____
Friday	⭐ ⭐	_____

Spelling Words

gave	use
time	most
cute	find
cone	she

What Happened Today? Write about one thing you did each day.

Monday _____

_____

Tuesday _____

_____

Wednesday _____

_____

Thursday _____

_____

Friday _____

_____

Keeping Track Color a book for every 10 minutes you read.

Monday	Tuesday	Wednesday	Thursday	Friday

My favorite book this week was

_____

I liked it because _____

_____

_____

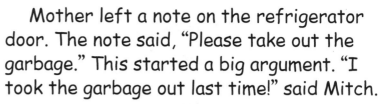

Take Out the Garbage

Please take out the garbage! Love, Mom

Mother left a note on the refrigerator door. The note said, "Please take out the garbage." This started a big argument. "I took the garbage out last time!" said Mitch.

"No, you didn't. I took it out when you stayed overnight at Pete's house!" shouted Marcus.

"Wait a minute, you two. Fighting won't help," said their older brother when he heard the boys arguing. "Let's do it together. First we have to take out the cans, plastic, and glass and put them in the recycling bins."

As the boys worked, Marcus asked, "What happens to the garbage that isn't recycled?" Jerome explained that the rest of the garbage was taken to the landfill.

"I'll take you there some day so you can see what happens to the stuff we throw away," promised Jerome.

1. Why were the boys arguing? don't

   Because they ~~always~~ want to take out the trash

2. What did Jerome suggest that they do?

   take it out together

3. Where does the garbage that is not recycled go?

   It can only take paper and paper stuff

Plastic   Glass   Paper

Monday

Week 2

(23)

Write It Right

1. mom was make cookies for my lunch

Mom was making cookies for my lunch.

2. them girls was playing a game

The girls were playing a game.

3. how many cows was in the farmers barn

How many cows were in the farmers barn?

MATH TIME

Name the shapes.

square	cone	circle
triangle	pyramid	rectangle
sphere	cube	hexagon

triangle

cube

square

pyramid

rectangle

cone

Hexagon

circle

©2005 by Evan-Moor Corp. • Daily Summer Activities 2-3 • EMC 1029

Spell It!

Unscramble the letters.

gave   use   time   most
cute   find   cone   she

1. dnif _find_
2. ceno _cone_
3. vage _gave_
4. stom _most_
5. meti _time_
6. sue _use_
7. tuce _cute_
8. hes _she_

Write sentences using the spelling words that have a long i.

1. I will find you!

2. Oh my gosh the time is 9:00 am

Use your best handwriting as you write the capital letters.

A B C D E F G H I J K L M
N O P Q R S T U V W X Y Z

ABCDEFGHIGKLMNOPQRSTUVWXYZ

Tuesday   Week 2

Popcorn is a compound word.
Underline the compound words in these sentences.

1. My grandmother rides a motorcycle.

2. A butterfly landed on a flower in my backyard.

3. Will you make me pancakes with strawberry jam?

4. Marybeth saw a gopher disappear underground.

Match words to make compound words. Write the new words on the lines.

honey	girl	_____
dragon	sauce	_____
cow	fly	_____
apple	bee	_____

MATH TIME

Add and subtract.

73	23	89	61	18	76	37	10
+ 15	- 12	- 35	+ 23	+ 11	- 32	- 30	+ 30

64	15	58	52	11	25	12	96
- 31	+ 14	- 11	+ 32	+ 73	- 12	+ 24	- 40

42	38	65	39	43	61	44	75
+ 36	+ 21	- 31	- 27	- 12	+ 25	+ 54	- 31

©2005 by Evan-Moor Corp. • Daily Summer Activities 2-3 • EMC 1029

Where Does the Garbage Go?

Have you ever wondered what happens to your garbage after it is collected?

Garbage is picked up by trucks and taken to landfills away from towns and cities. Landfills are gigantic holes in the ground. The soil is packed hard. Then special liners are put in the holes to keep garbage from seeping into nearby soil.

Garbage trucks dump their loads into the landfill. Workers at the landfill use bulldozers to mash and pile the garbage into level layers. Each day the garbage is covered with a layer of soil.

1. What is a landfill?

   giganic holes in the ground

2. How does the garbage get to the landfill?

   by a big truck

3. What happens to the garbage after it gets to the landfill?

   _____

4. Think of two ways that you can help make less garbage.

   _____   _____

Wednesday

Week 2

Language Bytes

Write each word below on the line next to its rhyming word.

tie	funny	bed	we	play	fly

stay ___play___

red ___bed___

sky ___fly___

pie ___tie___

key ___we___

honey ___funny___

Circle the two words that rhyme in each sentence.

1. There were ten chickens in the pen.

2. Uncle Elton spilled apple pie on his new tie.

3. Where did the nurse keep her purse at the hospital?

MATH TIME

Write the correct sign in each circle.

6 < 9   4 = 4   8 > 2

12 > 9   100 < 101   299 > 199

31 > 13   144 > 414   500 > 300

46 < 64   263 > 236   230 = 230

90 > 60   246 = 246   461 < 473

70 < 77   689 < 890   902 < 920

©2005 by Evan-Moor Corp. • Daily Summer Activities 2-3 • EMC 1029

Ge⊛graphy

Color the water blue.
Color the land green.

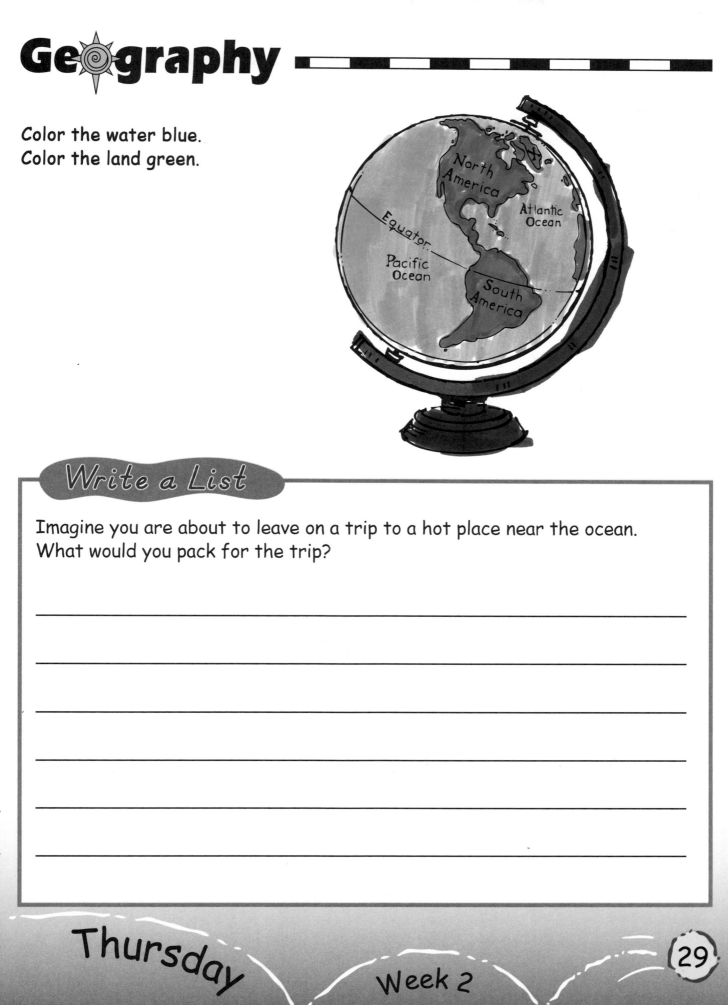

Write a List

Imagine you are about to leave on a trip to a hot place near the ocean.
What would you pack for the trip?

_____

_____

_____

_____

_____

MATH TIME

Count the money.

1. ___25___ ¢

3. _____ ¢

2. _____ ¢

4. $ _____

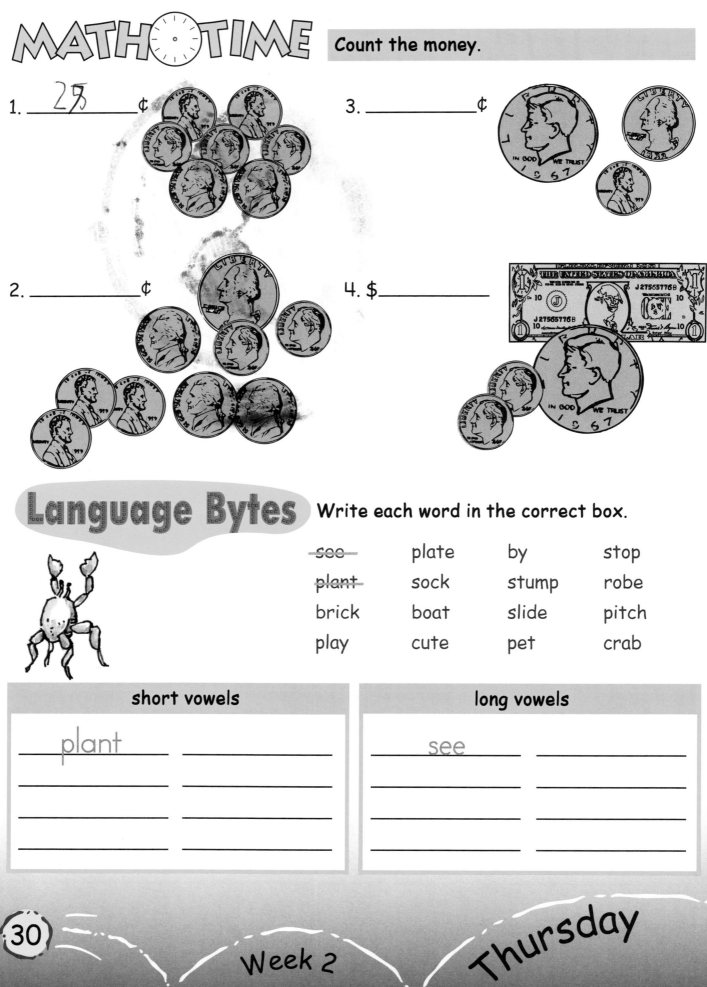

Language Bytes

Write each word in the correct box.

~~see~~	plate	by	stop
~~plant~~	sock	stump	robe
brick	boat	slide	pitch
play	cute	pet	crab

short vowels	long vowels
plant _____	see _____
_____ _____	_____ _____
_____ _____	_____ _____
_____ _____	_____ _____

©2005 by Evan-Moor Corp. • Daily Summer Activities 2-3 • EMC 1029

Language Bytes

Circle the words that name something (nouns).

funny	puppy	swim	table
robin	plane	corn	hard
woman	purple	spider	bicycle
speedy	huge	gorilla	uncle
ice cream	unhappy	building	tiny

MATH TIME

Find the answers.

1. Isaac went to the ball game at 3:00. He came home at 7:00. How long was he gone?

_____ hours

2. Mrs. Johansen won three yellow ribbons, seven red ribbons, and four blue ribbons at the county fair. How many ribbons did she win?

_____ ribbons

3. Tanisha saw 8 cows, 9 hens, and 6 sheep at her uncle's farm. How many farm animals did she see?

farm
_____ animals

4. Ernesto has 35 cents. If he spends a quarter on candy, how much money will he have left?

_____ cents

Friday

Week 2

(31)

Use the code to solve the riddle.

1 - a	5 - e	9 - i	13 - m	17 - q	21 - u	25 - y
2 - b	6 - f	10 - j	14 - n	18 - r	22 - v	26 - z
3 - c	7 - g	11 - k	15 - o	19 - s	23 - w	
4 - d	8 - h	12 - l	16 - p	20 - t	24 - x	

What is black and white and red all over?

$\underline{\text{a}}$ $\underline{\hphantom{xx}}$ $\underline{\hphantom{xx}}$ $\underline{\hphantom{xx}}$ $\underline{\hphantom{xx}}$ $\underline{\hphantom{xx}}$ $\underline{\hphantom{xx}}$ $\underline{\hphantom{xx}}$

1   16   5   14   7   21   9   14

23   9   20   8   1

19   21   14   2   21   18   14 !

Circle the answer.

On another sheet of paper, write your favorite riddle in code.

©2005 by Evan-Moor Corp. • Daily Summer Activities 2-3 • EMC 1029

Color a ⭐ for each page finished.

Parent's Initials

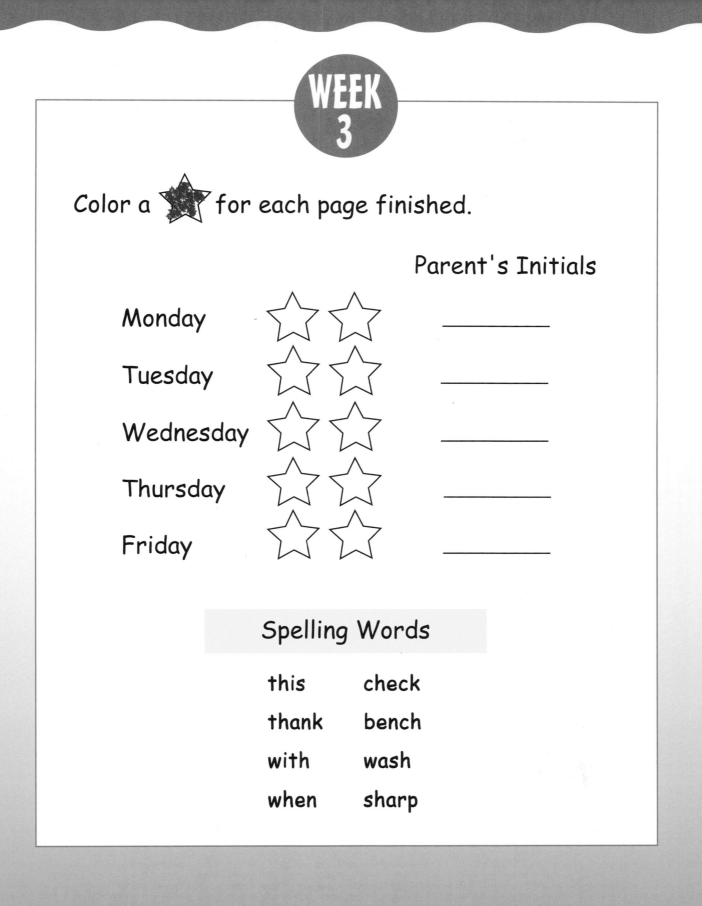

Monday

Tuesday

Wednesday

Thursday

Friday

_____

_____

_____

_____

_____

Spelling Words

this	check
thank	bench
with	wash
when	sharp

What Happened Today? Write about one thing you did each day.

Monday _____

_____

Tuesday _____

_____

Wednesday _____

_____

Thursday _____

_____

Friday _____

_____

Keeping Track Color a book for every 10 minutes you read.

Monday	Tuesday	Wednesday	Thursday	Friday

My favorite book this week was

_____

I liked it because _____

_____

_____

An Elephant Poem

Way down south
    where bananas grow
A grasshopper stepped
    on an elephant's toe.
The elephant cried
    with tears in his eyes,
"Pick on somebody
    your own size!"

Anonymous

1. Where does this poem take place?

way down south

2. Why is the elephant crying?

A grasshopper stepped on his toe

3. Do you think a grasshopper could hurt an elephant by stepping on its foot? Why?

I

4. Write something in this poem that could be real and something that is make-believe.

real: U

make-believe: _____

5. This poem is by Anonymous. What does that mean?

_____

Write It Right

1. at what time does she party begin

_____

2. he gived the toy to kim

_____

3. dont touch that broken glass

_____

MATH TIME

Find the answers.

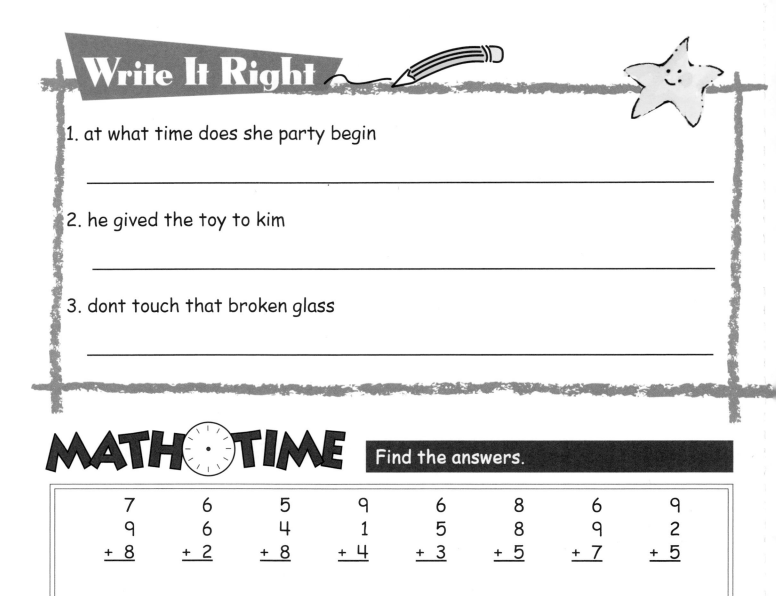

7	6	5	9	6	8	6	9
9	6	4	1	5	8	9	2
+ 8	+ 2	+ 8	+ 4	+ 3	+ 5	+ 7	+ 5

35	44	13	23	30	52	21	24
24	12	22	42	34	15	12	22
+ 10	+ 41	+ 12	+ 21	+ 32	+ 22	+ 34	+ 41

23	31	22	25	32	63	40	18
43	50	53	42	34	13	12	20
+ 20	+ 17	+ 12	+ 31	+ 32	+ 22	+ 34	+ 61

©2005 by Evan-Moor Corp. • Daily Summer Activities 2-3 • EMC 1029

Language Bytes

Fill in the missing letters.

th ch wh sh

___this   wi_th_   _sh_arp   wa_th_

ben_ch_   _wh_en   _ch_eck   ___ank

Use the spelling words to complete the sentences.

1. I _____ I had a little bunny _____ a pink nose.

2. That knife is very _____.

3. Dad wrote a _____ to pay for my new shoes.

4. Sit on that _____ and rest if you are tired.

Copy this poem using your best handwriting.

Gray, wrinkled, saggy skin
That's the cover an elephant's in.

Match the words that have the same meaning.

1. large	yell	6. wee	see
2. sad	smile	7. mean	tiny
3. shout	gift	8. look	empty
4. grin	unhappy	9. quick	unkind
5. present	huge	10. hollow	fast

MATH TIME

Ones - Tens - Hundreds

479
hundreds   tens   ones

1. Circle the number in the ones place.

45   67   90   125   302   63   289   106

2. Circle the number in the tens place.

39   52   81   163   280   96   374   139

3. Circle the number in the hundreds place.

163   489   204   335   602   232   385   115

4. Write the number.

2 tens = _____   3 hundreds = _____

6 ones = _____   1 hundred = _____

9 tens = _____   5 hundreds = _____

38

Week 3

Tuesday

©2005 by Evan-Moor Corp. • Daily Summer Activities 2-3 • EMC 1029

An Elephant's Trunk

An elephant's trunk is amazing. The trunk is the elephant's nose. It is used for breathing and smelling, but it has other uses, too.

An elephant eats several hundred pounds of grass, fruit, branches, twigs, and leaves every day. The elephant uses its trunk to gather the food and put it into its mouth. The trunk has a fingerlike tip that helps to pick up food.

The elephant also uses its trunk when it drinks. The elephant sucks water up into its trunk the way you would use a straw. Then the elephant blows the water into its mouth. The elephant uses its trunk to collect water when it takes a bath, too. It sucks up water and then blows it out all over its body.

1. List four ways an elephant uses its trunk.

_____

_____

_____

_____

2. How is an elephant's trunk like your

nose? _____

hands? _____

©2005 by Evan-Moor Corp. • Daily Summer Activities 2-3 • EMC 1029

Language Bytes

Write the long vowel sound you hear in each word.

1. make ___a___
2. kite _____
3. she _____
4. use _____
5. so _____

6. seen _____
7. cute _____
8. goat _____
9. flea _____
10. pie _____

11. try _____
12. play _____
13. high _____
14. toe _____
15. eight_____

MATH TIME

Find the answers.

1. Mr. Stern bought satin ribbons for his daughters.
   He got 12 each of blue, yellow, green, and red.
   How many ribbons did he buy?   _____ ribbons

2. There were 25 children swimming in the pool.
   Then 13 got out of the pool. How many were
   still in the water?   _____ children

3. Maria wanted an ice-cream cone with two scoops
   of ice cream. A scoop of ice cream is 40¢, and
   a cone is 15¢. How much will it cost in all?   _____¢

4. What is half of 12?
   How did you get the answer?   _____

   _____

   _____

40

Week 3

Wednesday

©2005 by Evan-Moor Corp. • Daily Summer Activities 2-3 • EMC 1029

Geography

Write the four directions in the correct places on this map.

north	south	east	west

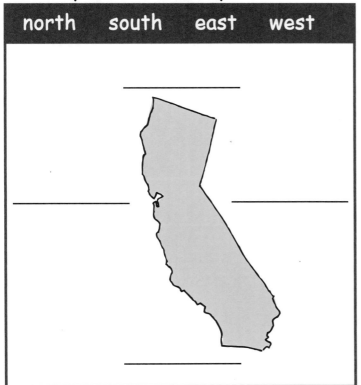

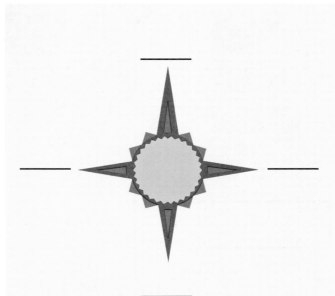

Write **N**, **S**, **E**, and **W** in the correct places to show north, south, east, and west on this compass rose.

Read the chart, then write about elephants.

Elephants

weigh 8 tons

big ears

long trunk

thick, wrinkled skin

tusks

_____

_____

_____

_____

_____

_____

Thursday

Week 3

MATH⏰TIME

fourth	second	sixth
third	fifth	first

Language Bytes

Number the sentences in order to tell a story.

_____ Nan paid for their tickets.

_____ The children walked up to the ticket counter.

_____ Father drove Alex and Nan to the theater.

_____ Alex and Nan watched the show.

_____ Father came to pick up the children and take them home.

Week 3

Thursday

©2005 by Evan-Moor Corp. • Daily Summer Activities 2–3 • EMC 1029

Language Bytes

Where does the apostrophe belong?

| Barbara's pony | three dogs' bones |

1. Tammys toy kangaroo
2. Davids new sneakers
3. Marks skateboard
4. two rabbits carrots
5. both girls dance slippers

6. all the parents cars
7. both second-graders teacher
8. Amys two dogs
9. my neighbor's fence
10. a firefighters truck

MATH TIME

Count by 2s.

2   4   ___   ___   ___   ___   18   ___

22   ___   ___   ___   34   ___   ___   ___

___   46   ___   ___   ___   ___   ___

___   ___   ___   72   ___   ___   ___

___   84   ___   ___   ___   ___   ___

Friday

Week 3

Read the clues to complete the crossword puzzle.

Animals from Africa

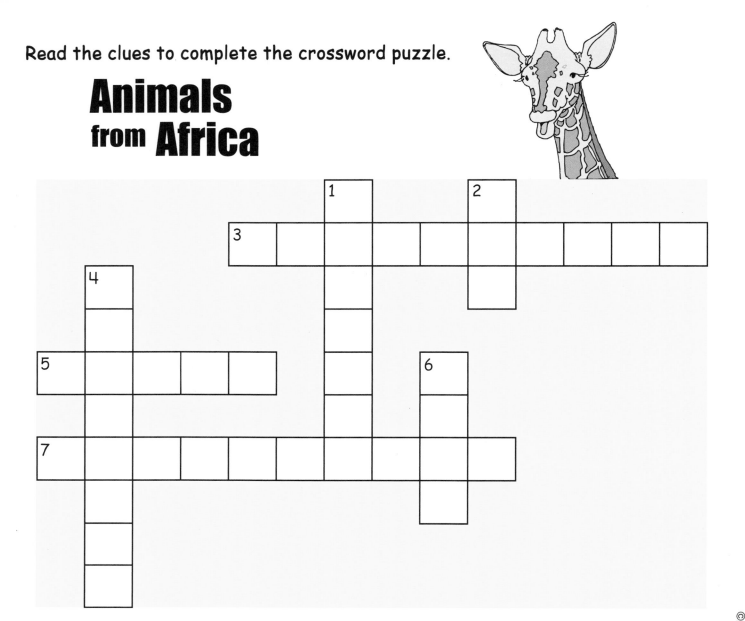

Across
3. a large ape with humanlike eyes and ears
5. a horselike animal with black-and-white stripes
7. a large animal with thick skin and two horns on its snout

Down
1. a tall animal with long legs and a very long neck
2. it's not a bird, but it can fly
4. a huge animal with big ears and a long trunk
6. a large wildcat

Word Box
bat

chimpanzee

elephant

giraffe

lion

rhinoceros

zebra

©2005 by Evan-Moor Corp. • Daily Summer Activities 2-3 • EMC 1029

Week 3   Friday

Color a ⭐ for each page finished.

Parent's Initials

Monday	☆ ☆	_____
Tuesday	☆ ☆	_____
Wednesday	☆ ☆	_____
Thursday	☆ ☆	_____
Friday	☆ ☆	_____

Spelling Words

cake	rain
awake	paint
play	wait
today	eight

What Happened Today? Write about one thing you did each day.

Monday _____
_____

Tuesday _____
_____

Wednesday _____
_____

Thursday _____
_____

Friday _____
_____

Keeping Track Color a book for every 10 minutes you read.

Monday	Tuesday	Wednesday	Thursday	Friday

My favorite book this week was

_____

I liked it because _____
_____
_____

Little Red and the Wolf

A little redheaded girl was skipping along a path through the woods when she met a wolf. The wolf asked the little girl where she was going. Little Red remembered what her mother always said: "Don't talk to strangers." She quickly walked away from the wolf.

Little Red looked around. She saw her friend the woodcutter chopping down a tree. She ran to the woodcutter and told him about the wolf.

The woodcutter chased the wolf away and then walked Little Red to Grandma's house.

Grandma thanked the woodcutter for helping Little Red and invited him to stay for lunch.

1. Where was Little Red going when she met the wolf?

   _____

2. Tell two smart things Little Red did when she met the wolf.

   _____

   _____

3. How did Grandma thank the woodcutter for helping Little Red?

   _____

4. What would you do if a stranger tried to talk to you?

   _____

   _____

Monday

Write It Right

1. my uncle send a letter to bob and i

_____

2. does dr cruz work in portland

_____

3. next friday angela is going to the dentist

_____

MATH TIME

Add and subtract.

73	40	38	61	44	37	64	34
+ 8	− 7	− 8	+ 9	+ 7	− 6	+ 9	+ 5
54	92	36	47	93	50	44	58
− 25	− 53	+ 38	+ 23	− 24	− 16	+ 20	− 39
84	53	27	72	55	70	50	45
+ 19	− 18	− 10	+ 16	+ 25	− 58	+ 50	+ 36

©2005 by Evan-Moor Corp. • Daily Summer Activities 2-3 • EMC 1029

Spell It!

Write the letters that make the sound of a in each word.

a-e	ay	ai	eigh

1. pl_____

2. aw_____k_____

3. r_____n

4. _____t

5. tod_____

6. w_____t

7. p_____nt

8. c_____k_____

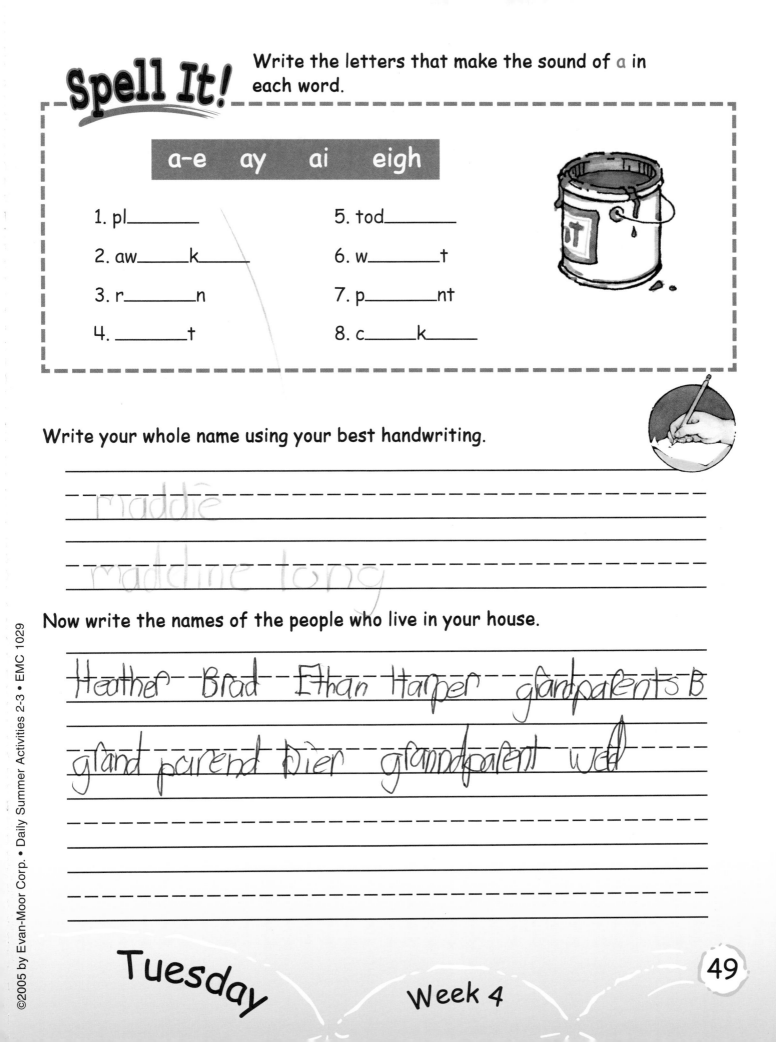

Write your whole name using your best handwriting.

maddie

maddie tong

Now write the names of the people who live in your house.

Heather Brad Ethan Harper grandparents B

grand parend bier granndparent wel

©2005 by Evan-Moor Corp. • Daily Summer Activities 2-3 • EMC 1029

Write the correct word.

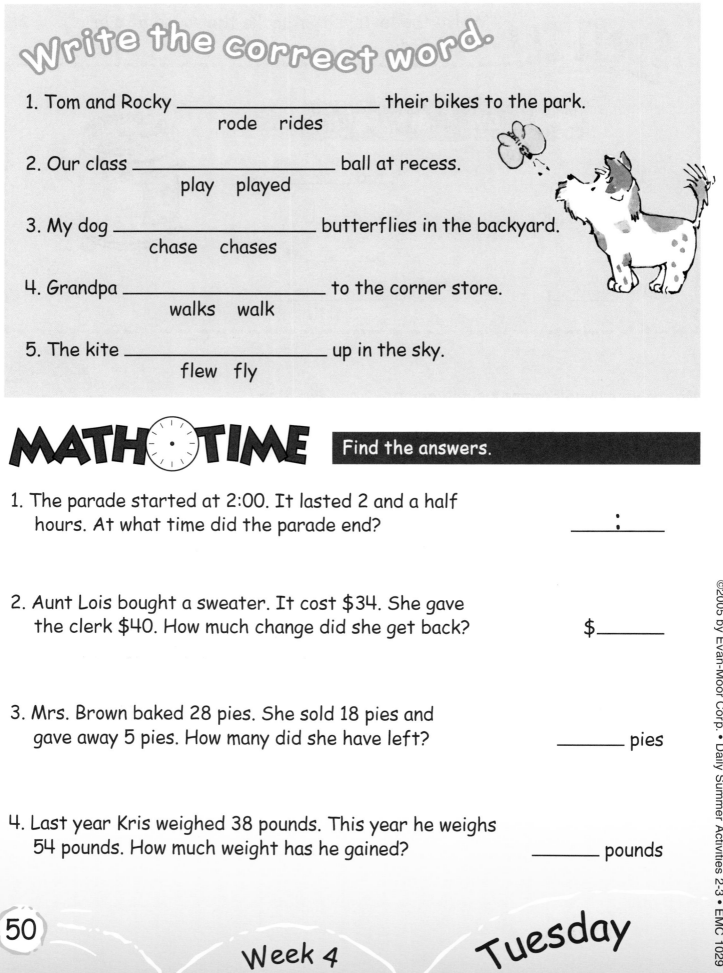

1. Tom and Rocky _____ their bikes to the park.
   rode   rides

2. Our class _____ ball at recess.
   play   played

3. My dog _____ butterflies in the backyard.
   chase   chases

4. Grandpa _____ to the corner store.
   walks   walk

5. The kite _____ up in the sky.
   flew   fly

MATH○TIME

Find the answers.

1. The parade started at 2:00. It lasted 2 and a half hours. At what time did the parade end?

   _____ : _____

2. Aunt Lois bought a sweater. It cost $34. She gave the clerk $40. How much change did she get back?

   $_____

3. Mrs. Brown baked 28 pies. She sold 18 pies and gave away 5 pies. How many did she have left?

   _____ pies

4. Last year Kris weighed 38 pounds. This year he weighs 54 pounds. How much weight has he gained?

   _____ pounds

©2005 by Evan-Moor Corp. • Daily Summer Activities 2-3 • EMC 1029

Do your parents have a lot of rules for you to remember? Are they always telling you to buckle your seat belt or not to talk to strangers?

Parents want to be sure their children are safe and healthy. Their rules are a way to remind children about what they should and should not do. How many things in this list are rules in your house? Underline them.

1. Look both ways before you cross the street.

2. Buckle your seat belt when you ride in a car.

3. Wear a safety helmet when you ride your bike.

4. Don't talk to or take gifts from strangers.

5. Wear a life jacket when you are in a boat.

Make a list of the safety rules in your house.

_____

_____

_____

_____

_____

_____

Language Bytes

Match each word with its opposite.

| sad | wet | cry | day | large |
| play | sit | fast | full | dirty |

1. slow _____

2. tiny _____

3. happy _____

4. work _____

5. night _____

6. empty _____

7. stand _____

8. dry _____

9. laugh _____

10. clean _____

MATH TIME

Read the graph to find the answers.

Hair Colors in Room 6

1. What color hair do most of the people have?

_____

2. How many people have:

black hair? _____

blond hair? _____

brown hair? _____

3. Do more people have red hair or gray hair?

_____

4. How many more people have brown hair than black hair?

_____

Week 4

Wednesday

©2005 by Evan-Moor Corp. • Daily Summer Activities 2-3 • EMC 1029

Ge✹graphy

There is an imaginary line around the middle of the Earth. It is called the equator. The equator divides the Earth in half. Each half is called a hemisphere. Land north of the equator is in the Northern Hemisphere. Land south of the equator is in the Southern Hemisphere.

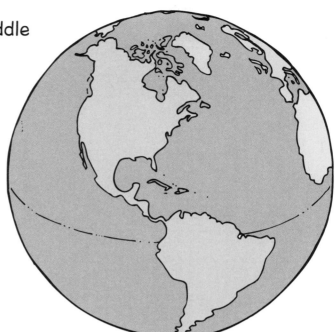

1. Trace the equator in red.

2. Make an X on the hemisphere where you live.

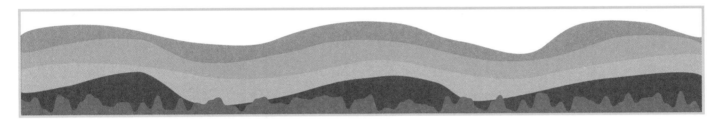

Write a story. Use another sheet of paper if you need more room.

One day as I was walking through the woods, _____

_____

_____

_____

_____

_____

Thursday

Week 4

Place values

20 + 7 = 27	100 + 30 + 2 = 132
2 tens + 7 ones = 27	1 hundred + 3 tens + 2 ones = 132

1. 10 + 8 = __18__

2. 40 + 5 = _____

3. 60 + 0 = __60__

4. 100 + 90 + 7 = __197__

5. 200 + 20 + 5 = __225__

6. 200 + 8 = _____

7. 5 tens + 3 ones = _____

8. 1 ten + 9 ones = _____

9. 8 tens + 5 ones = _____

10. 1 hundred + 6 tens + 4 ones = _____

11. 2 hundreds + 1 ten + 2 ones = _____

12. 3 hundreds + 8 tens = _____

Language Bytes

What does each contraction mean?

1. aren't __are not__

2. I'll __I will__

3. we're __we are__

4. I'm _____

5. isn't _____

6. don't _____

Write the correct contraction on each line.

1. That _____ his dog.

2. _____ fix it for you.

3. I _____ know how to bake a cake.

4. _____ going to have a party.

Language Bytes

Draw a circle around who or what the sentence is about.
Draw a line under what happened.

(The cowboy) rode a horse.

1. My ice-cream cone fell on the ground.

2. Dad and Uncle Mark went fishing.

3. Her cat had three kittens.

4. The rain got my hair wet.

5. The band played loud music.

6. Zelda painted a beautiful picture.

MATH TIME

How far is it around each shape?

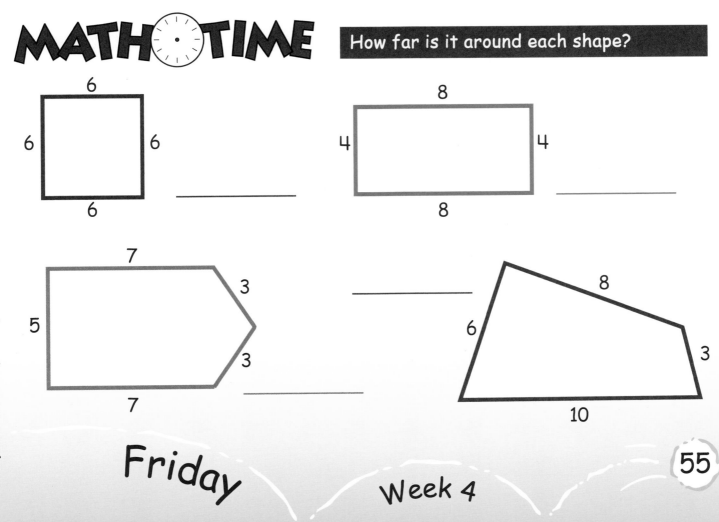

Find a path through the woods for Little Red.

Color the boxes as you count by 5s.

5	10	15	40	15	20
30	40	20	25	30	15
70	50	65	70	35	65
80	55	50	45	40	15
65	60	75	80	85	90
70	140	110	105	100	95
75	80	85	90	95	100
135	140	145	195	155	105
160	175	170	165	130	110
140	135	130	125	120	115
145	170	115	135	95	105
150	155	160	165	170	175

©2005 by Evan-Moor Corp. • Daily Summer Activities 2-3 • EMC 1029

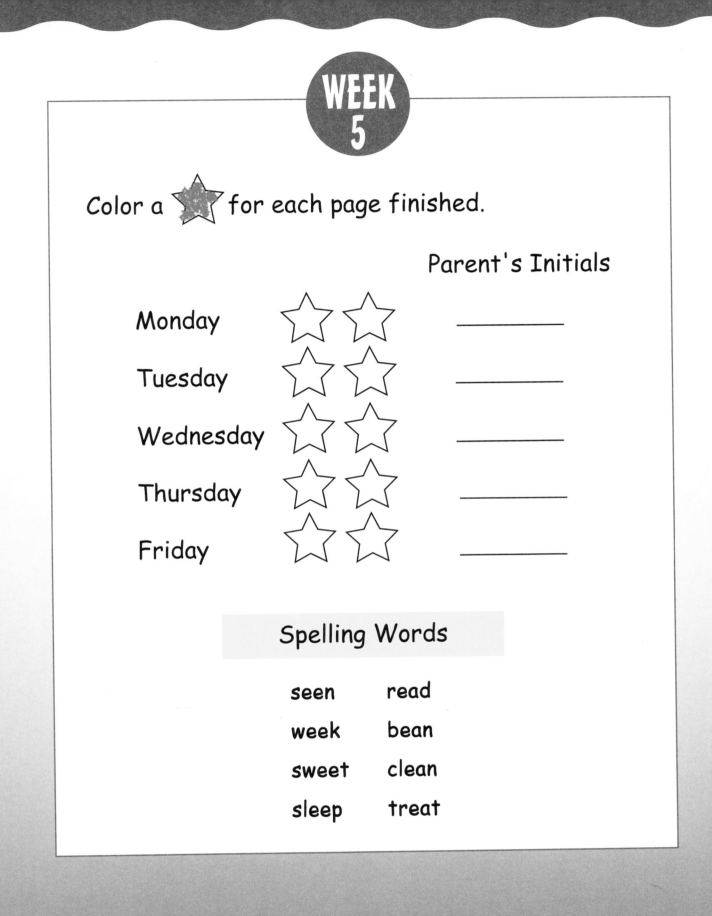

Color a ⭐ for each page finished.

Parent's Initials

Monday	☆ ☆	_____
Tuesday	☆ ☆	_____
Wednesday	☆ ☆	_____
Thursday	☆ ☆	_____
Friday	☆ ☆	_____

Spelling Words

seen	read
week	bean
sweet	clean
sleep	treat

What Happened Today? Write about one thing you did each day.

Monday _____

_____

Tuesday _____

_____

Wednesday _____

_____

Thursday _____

_____

Friday _____

_____

Keeping Track Color a book for every 10 minutes you read.

Monday	Tuesday	Wednesday	Thursday	Friday

My favorite book this week was

_____

I liked it because _____

_____

_____

A Surprise in the Bathtub

Ginny had been making mud pies in the backyard all afternoon. "You're a mess, kiddo!" said her dad. "It's into the bathtub with you."

"Dad!" screamed Ginny. "Come quick! There's a spider in the bathtub!"

Dad came and took a look. "You don't have to be afraid. It's not a harmful spider."

"I'm not afraid," explained Ginny. "I know it won't hurt me. I don't want it to drown when I turn on the water." Dad helped Ginny gently scoop the spider into a glass. They took the spider to the backyard and let it go. Ginny finally took a bath.

1. Why did her dad tell Ginny she was a mess?

_____

2. What did Ginny's dad mean when he said the spider was not harmful?

_____

3. Why did Ginny want to get the spider out of the bathtub?

_____

Monday   Week 5   59

Write It Right

1. were going to canada in july

_____

2. we don't have no sisters

_____

3. kelly peter and mike goed to the zoo

_____

MATH TIME   Multiplication

2 x 3 = _____   3 x 4 = _____   1 x 4 = _____

2 x 1 = _____   2 x 2 = _____   5 x 3 = _____

4 x 4 = _____   3 x 1 = _____   0 x 2 = _____

4 x 2 = _____   3 x 0 = _____   5 x 1 = _____

3 x 5 = _____   4 x 3 = _____   3 x 5 = _____

4	3	1	1	5	3	2	5
x 5	x 2	x 2	x 1	x 2	x 3	x 4	x 5

©2005 by Evan-Moor Corp. • Daily Summer Activities 2-3 • EMC 1029

Spell It!
Circle the words that are spelled correctly.

1. dera   read   5. seen   nese
2. week   kewe   6. celan   clean
3. naeb   bean   7. twees   sweet
4. sleep   peles   8. treat   retat

Write a sentence using the spelling words that rhyme with meet.

1. _____

2. _____

Copy this poem using your best handwriting.

I saw a spider start to spin
A spider web to go hunting in.
She used three pairs of spinnerets
Creating beautiful sticky nets.

CAPITAL LETTERS

The names of people, pets, and places begin with capital letters. Copy the words. Use a capital letter where it is needed.

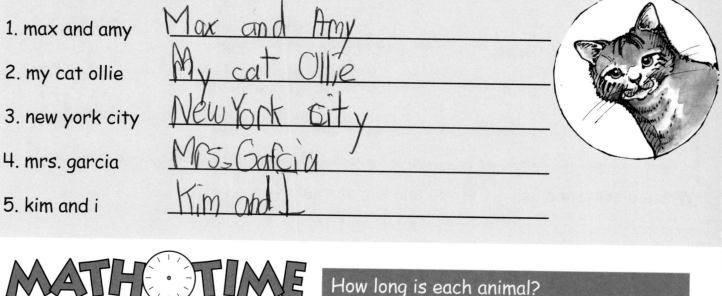

1. max and amy   Max and Amy

2. my cat ollie   My cat Ollie

3. new york city   New York City

4. mrs. garcia   Mrs. Garcia

5. kim and i   Kim and I

MATH TIME

How long is each animal?

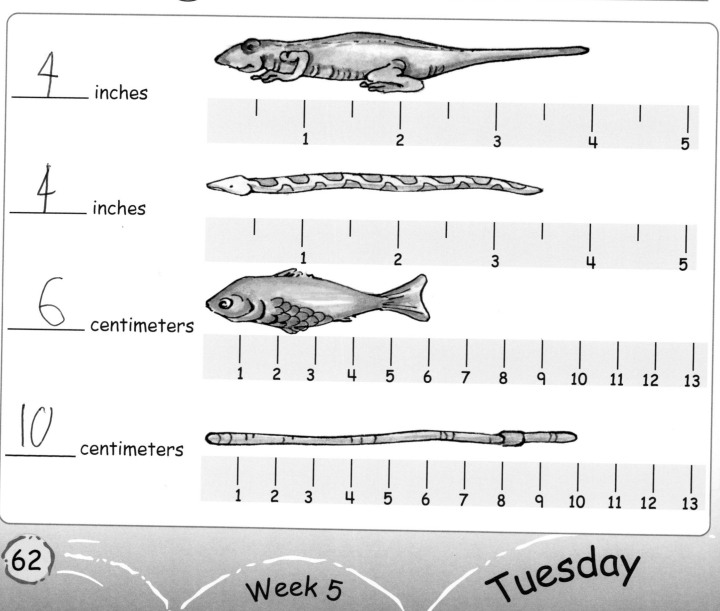

4 inches

4 inches

6 centimeters

10 centimeters

©2005 by Evan-Moor Corp. • Daily Summer Activities 2-3 • EMC 1029

Spiders

What has eight legs and can spin silk?

Answer: A spider!

There are thousands of kinds of spiders. They are different shapes, sizes, and colors. They live in different places. But all spiders are alike in these ways:

Spiders have eight legs.

Spiders have a hard outer skeleton.

Spiders have two main body parts.

Spiders spin silk threads from spinnerets.

Spiders use silk webs to help catch food. Some spiders use silk threads to move through the air from one place to another. Spiders that live underground line their homes with silk. There is even a spider that lives in the water inside a home made of silk.

Spiders may look scary, but only a few kinds are harmful to humans. Most spiders are helpful because they eat insects.

1. How are all spiders the same?

_____

_____

2. In what ways do spiders use their silk?

_____

3. How are spiders helpful?

_____

Language Bytes

Read each sentence. Write a word to show ownership. Don't forget the apostrophe!

1. The dog belongs to Toby.

_____ dog

2. The paints belong to the artist.

_____ paints

3. That truck belongs to the firefighters.

_____ truck

4. The toys belong to the children.

_____ toys

5. Those boots belong to the cowgirl.

_____ boots

MATH TIME

There are many ways to name a number.

five

★★★★★   5   8 – 3

4 + 1   less than 10

Think about the number 8. Show five ways to name it.

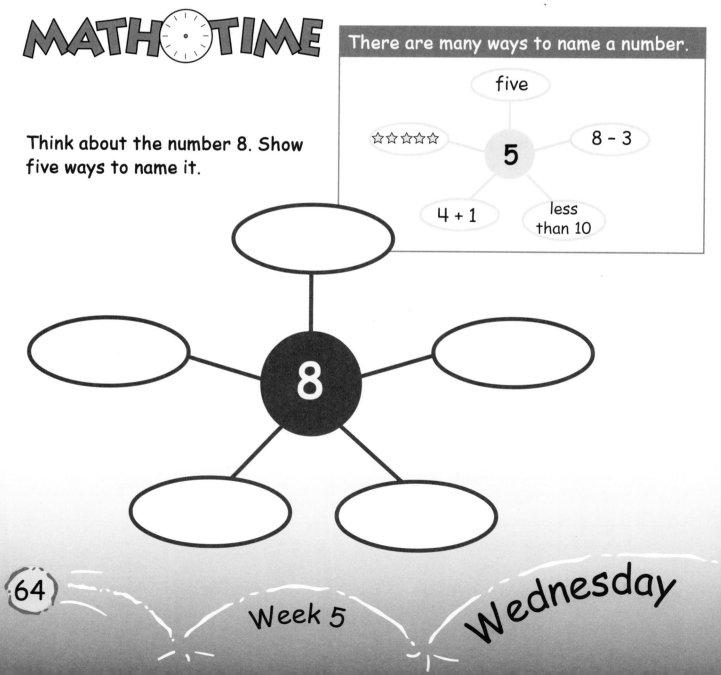

8

Geography

Use this map of North America to help you answer the questions.

1. Which country is north of the United States?

_____

2. Which country is south of the United States?

_____

3. Which country has more land— Canada or Mexico?

_____

4. Make an X on the Pacific Ocean. Make a ✔ on the Atlantic Ocean.

Pacific Ocean

Canada

United States

Mexico

Atlantic Ocean

N

W   E

S

What do you look like? Look at yourself in a mirror. Think about your hair, your eyes, and your face. Describe yourself.

_____

_____

_____

_____

_____

Thursday

Week 5

1. Chef Roy baked 4 birthday cakes.
   He put 8 candles on each cake.
   How many candles did he use?

   _____ candles

2. Jamal spent 85¢ on a muffin and 30¢ on milk.
   How much did his snack cost?

   $____.____

3. If one goat has 4 legs, how many legs will
   10 goats have?

   _____ legs

4. The farmer gathered 3 dozen eggs.
   How many did he gather?

   _____ eggs

Language Bytes

Underline what the speaker is saying.

Carlos said, "My tooth is loose."

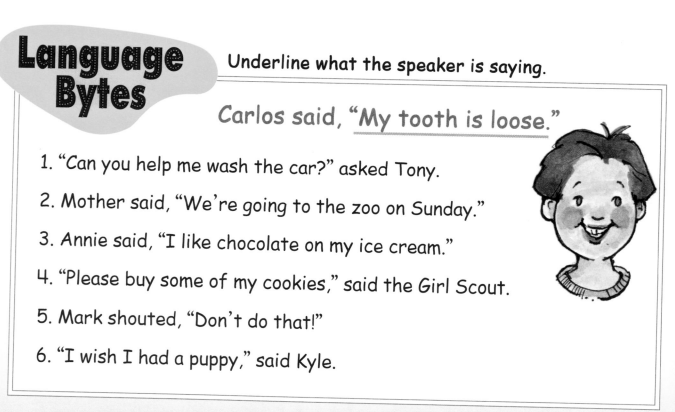

1. "Can you help me wash the car?" asked Tony.

2. Mother said, "We're going to the zoo on Sunday."

3. Annie said, "I like chocolate on my ice cream."

4. "Please buy some of my cookies," said the Girl Scout.

5. Mark shouted, "Don't do that!"

6. "I wish I had a puppy," said Kyle.

Week 5

Thursday

©2005 by Evan-Moor Corp. • Daily Summer Activities 2–3 • EMC 1029

Spell It!

Write an ending after each letter to make new words.
Read the words you made to someone.

old	g_____	m_____	s_____	f_____
and	b_____	h_____	s_____	st_____
ill	b_____	f_____	p_____	sp_____

Write the missing words.

1. Jack _____ the cow for a handful of beans.

2. We had to _____ in line a long time to buy tickets.

3. Try not to _____ your grape juice on the white rug.

MATH TIME

How many apples?

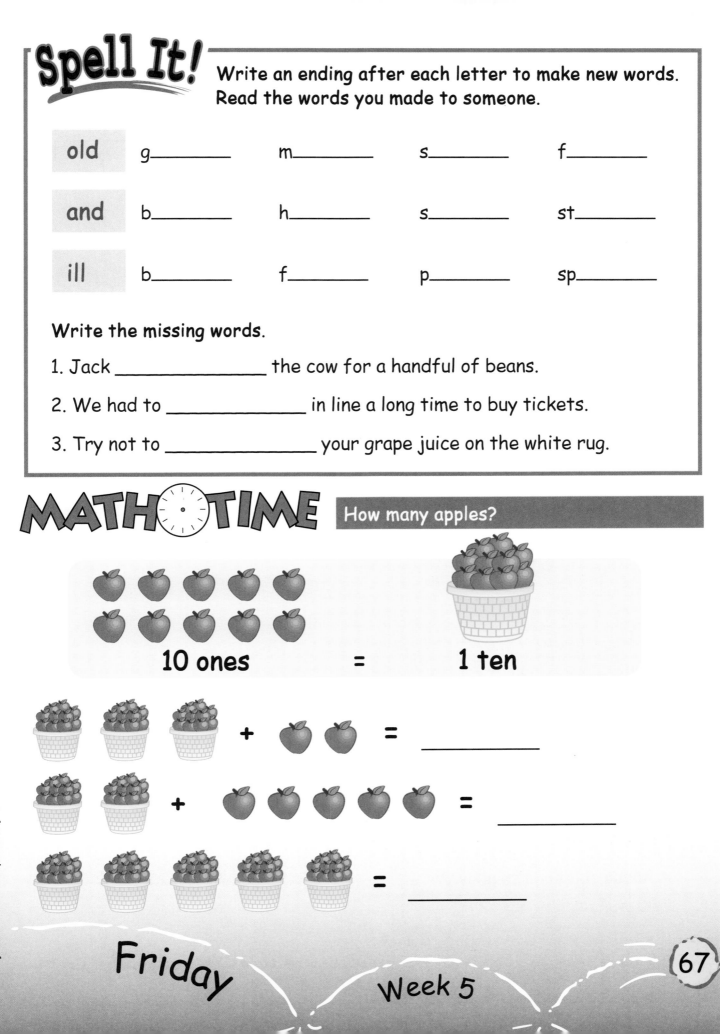

10 ones = 1 ten

$$+ \quad = \quad \underline{\hspace{2cm}}$$

$$+ \quad = \quad \underline{\hspace{2cm}}$$

$$= \quad \underline{\hspace{2cm}}$$

Friday

Week 5

67

Spiders

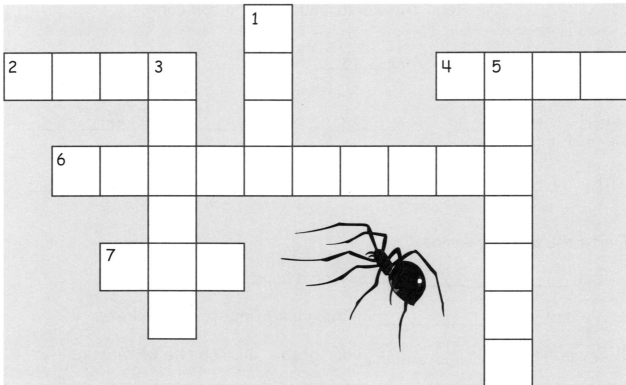

Across

2. baby spiders hatch from these
4. what webs are made of
6. the parts of a spider that make silk
7. a silk trap used to catch food

Down

1. how spiders make webs
3. a land animal with 8 legs
5. spiders eat these small animals

Use the clues to name these spiders.

A tarantula is a large hairy spider.

_____

A black widow is a shiny, black poisonous spider.

_____

A house spider is small with long legs.

_____

Color a ⭐ for each page finished.

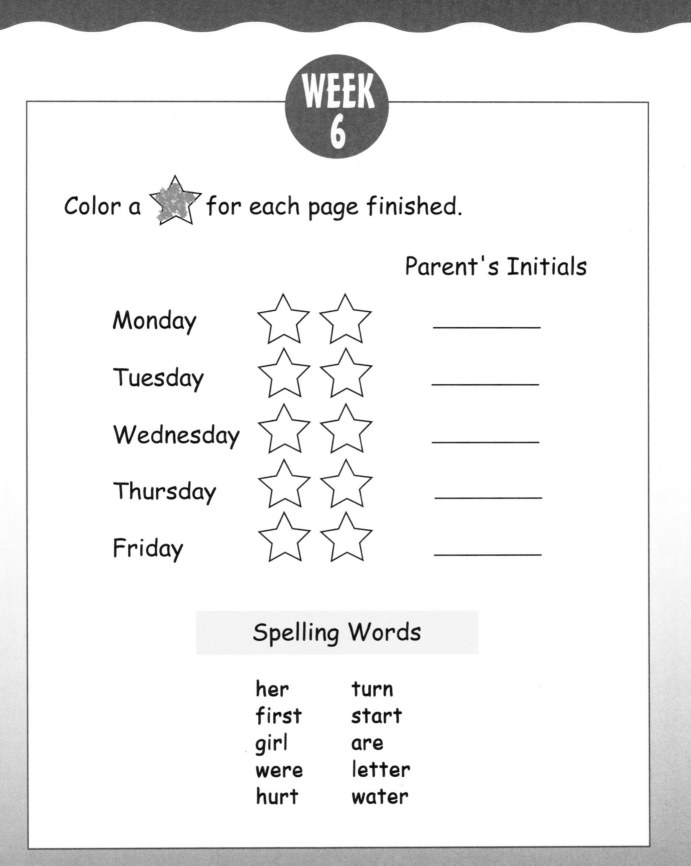

Parent's Initials

Monday ☆ ☆ _____

Tuesday ☆ ☆ _____

Wednesday ☆ ☆ _____

Thursday ☆ ☆ _____

Friday ☆ ☆ _____

Spelling Words

her	turn
first	start
girl	are
were	letter
hurt	water

What Happened Today? Write about one thing you did each day.

Monday _____

_____

Tuesday _____

_____

Wednesday _____

_____

Thursday _____

_____

Friday _____

_____

Keeping Track Color a book for every 10 minutes you read.

Monday	Tuesday	Wednesday	Thursday	Friday

My favorite book this week was

_____

I liked it because _____

_____

_____

Margo's Dream

I have always wanted to travel out in space. I dream about what it would feel like to be an astronaut leaving Earth. The countdown begins:

10, 9, 8, 7, 6, 5, 4, 3, 2, 1, blast off!

My ship rises from the launch pad. Up I go, higher and higher. What will I see as I travel across the solar system?

I look out. Earth and the moon shine in the black sky. They grow smaller and smaller as I move away.

I look across the sky. Stars twinkle. Meteors fly by. It's a long way between the planets, but I'm on my way.

Look out Mars. Here I come!

1. What has Margo always wanted to do?

_____

2. Where is she traveling in her dream?

_____

3. What does Margo see when she looks out the windows of the spaceship?

_____

4. Why do Earth and the moon look smaller and smaller?

_____

5. Would you like to travel across space? Why or why not?

_____

©2005 by Evan-Moor Corp. • Daily Summer Activities 2-3 • EMC 1029

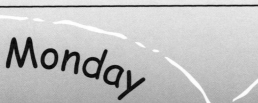

Monday

Week 6

Write It Right

1. there arent no fish in the bowl

_____

2. i want to ride anns bicycle

_____

3. what are mrs brown planting in her garden

_____

MATH TIME

Add and subtract.

21	30	58	74	43	87	52	31
+ 18	+ 9	- 24	- 30	+ 16	- 35	+ 46	+ 27

38	73	30	60	46	53	72	61
+ 2	+ 8	- 9	- 12	+ 14	+ 27	+ 19	+ 29

95	72	88	31	63	54	80	27
- 65	+ 19	+ 8	- 15	- 21	- 27	- 50	- 9

©2005 by Evan-Moor Corp. • Daily Summer Activities 2-3 • EMC 1029

Spell It!

Fill in the missing letters.

er   ir   ur   ar

1. h_er_   3. h____t   5. st____t

2. t____n   4. w____e   6. f____st

Circle the words that are spelled correctly.

1. ar   are   4. gril   girl   7. were   wur

2. her   hur   5. hurt   hert   8. frist   first

3. letter   lettar   6. trun   turn   9. start   sart

Copy this funny sentence to practice writing most of the letters of the alphabet. Use your best handwriting.

The quick brown fox jumped over the lazy dog.

_____

_____

_____

_____

What letter is missing in the sentence? _____

Language Bytes

Write each list in alphabetical order.

apple	1. _____
ostrich	2. _____
uncle	3. _____
egg	4. _____

whale	1. _____
weather	2. _____
won	3. _____
water	4. _____

cow	1. _____
clock	2. _____
castle	3. _____
cent	4. _____

harm	1. _____
hug	2. _____
house	3. _____
his	4. _____

MATH TIME   Find the answers.

1. Dad cooked 23 hamburgers for the picnic.
   If 19 hamburgers were eaten, how many
   hamburgers were left?   _____ hamburgers

2. Mary spent 20¢, Jill spent 25¢, and Ed spent 32¢.
   How much did they spend altogether?   _____¢

3. How many hippos are there if 11 are on the
   riverbank and 7 are in the water?   _____ hippos

4. A clown had 17 balloons. He gave 3 red balloons and
   6 blue balloons to children. How many did he have left?   _____ balloons

Mars

Mars is one of the nine planets in our solar system. It is the fourth planet from the Sun. It is 141 million miles (227 million kilometers) from the sun.

Mars is about half the size of Earth. It is a desert except for the ice caps at the north and south poles. Mars has tall mountains and deep canyons. The soil is full of rust-colored iron dust. This makes Mars look red. Strong winds blow up big storms of red dust.

It is very cold on Mars. This is because Mars doesn't have an atmosphere. There is no air to hold heat from the sun.

1. How many planets are in our solar system?

   _____

2. Why does Mars look red?

   _____

3. How much smaller is Mars than Earth?

   _____

4. Could you live on Mars? Explain your answer.

   _____

   _____

   _____

Write the correct homophones on the lines.

1. My _____ lives in New York City.

   A little black _____ bit my toe.

2. A strong wind _____ the man's hat off.

   Kim has new _____ shoes.

3. We _____ spaghetti for lunch.

   Tony's rabbit had _____ babies.

4. Where will you _____ on Saturday?

   A bumble_____ is fat and fuzzy.

ant
aunt

blew
blue

eight
ate

be
bee

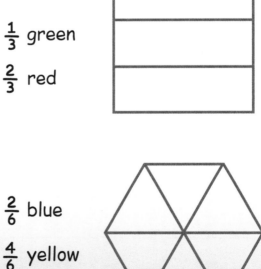

MATH TIME

Color each fraction.

$\frac{1}{2}$ brown

$\frac{1}{2}$ purple

$\frac{1}{3}$ green

$\frac{2}{3}$ red

$\frac{1}{4}$ yellow

$\frac{1}{4}$ blue

$\frac{2}{4}$ red

$\frac{2}{6}$ blue

$\frac{4}{6}$ yellow

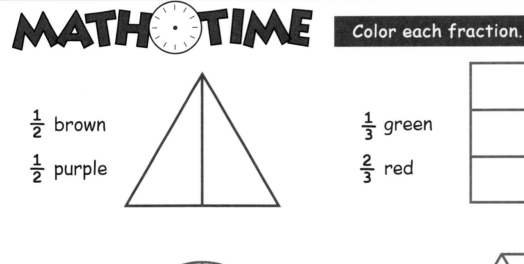

This map shows the seven continents.
Draw a circle around the continent on which you live.

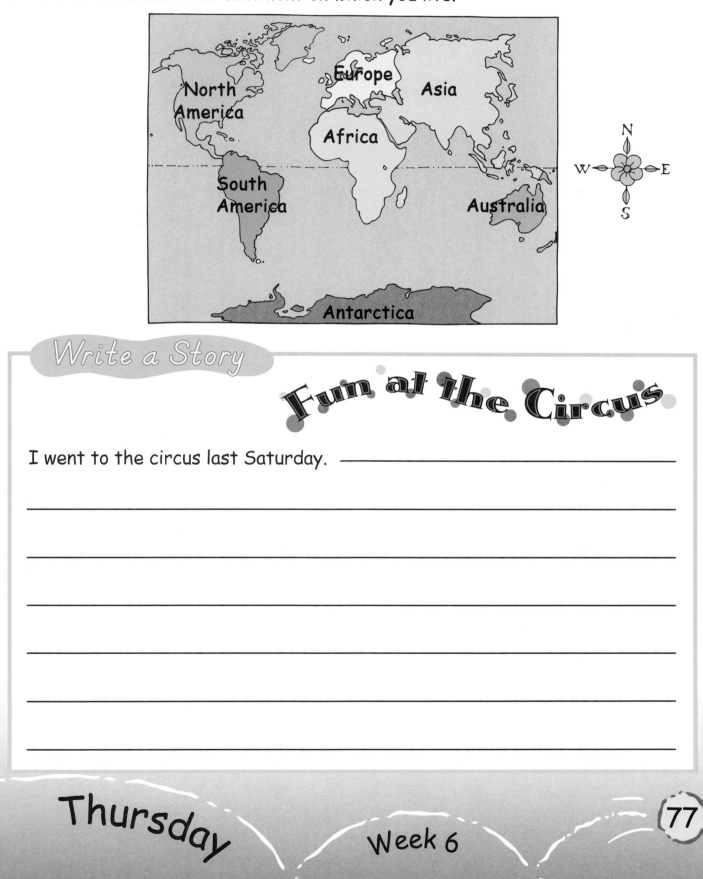

Write a Story

Fun at the Circus

I went to the circus last Saturday. _____

_____

_____

_____

_____

_____

MATH  TIME

_____:_____   _____ o'clock   half past _____

Draw hands on the clocks.

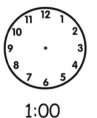

1:00   6:30   half past 8

 **Language Bytes**

An adjective describes something.
Circle the adjectives in the sentences below.

See the (big) (red) apple.

1. A small black dog played with an old red ball.

2. The ugly troll had big eyes and a long crooked nose.

3. One hot afternoon, a large lion slept in the cool shade of a tall tree.

4. Mark loved big crunchy cookies with cold milk.

5. The little green frog had smooth, moist skin.

Write six words that describe you.

_____   _____   _____

_____   _____   _____

Week 6   _Thursday_

©2005 by Evan-Moor Corp. • Daily Summer Activities 2-3 • EMC 1029

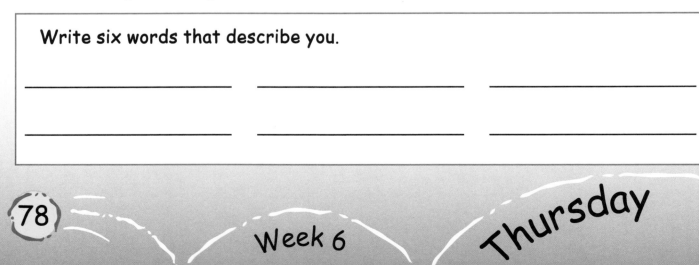

Write the words that go together in groups. Give each group a name.

whale	spoon	Mars	fork	jellyfish
shark	Pluto	octopus	star	Jupiter
Moon	knife	plate	tuna	glass

(group name)	(group name)	(group name)
1. _____	1. _____	1. _____
2. _____	2. _____	2. _____
3. _____	3. _____	3. _____
4. _____	4. _____	4. _____
5. _____	5. _____	5. _____

MATH TIME

Draw the shapes.

square	triangle	rectangle

How are the shapes alike?

_____

How are the shapes different?

_____

_____

Friday

Week 6

Connect the dots. Start at 300.

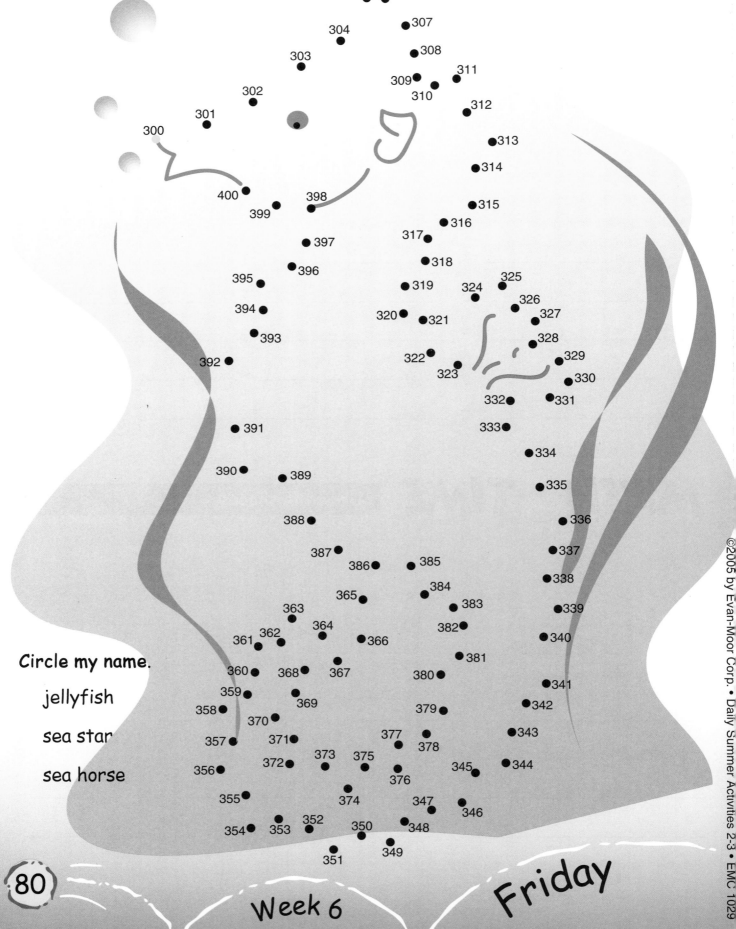

Circle my name.

jellyfish

sea star

sea horse

©2005 by Evan-Moor Corp. • Daily Summer Activities 2-3 • EMC 1029

Color a ⭐ for each page finished.

Parent's Initials

Monday ☆☆ _____

Tuesday ☆☆ _____

Wednesday ☆☆ _____

Thursday ☆☆ _____

Friday ☆☆ _____

Spelling Words

no	slow
toe	show
rose	coat
stone	goat
bow	float

What Happened Today? Write about one thing you did each day.

Monday _____
_____

Tuesday _____
_____

Wednesday _____
_____

Thursday _____
_____

Friday _____
_____

Keeping Track Color a book for every 10 minutes you read.

Monday	Tuesday	Wednesday	Thursday	Friday

My favorite book this week was

_____

I liked it because _____

_____

_____

Off We Go!

Elton and Beth flew to Memphis for a vacation. When the jet arrived, Aunt Sarah met the children. "How was your trip?" she asked.

"It was awesome!" said Elton. "We've never been on an airplane before. It was huge!"

"The flight attendant helped us find our seats and buckle up," said Beth. "It was kind of scary taking off, but then we had fun."

"We got to eat lunch and see a movie. And we took turns looking out the window," said Elton. "Have you ever flown in an airplane, Aunt Sarah?"

"No," answered Aunt Sarah. "But I will. I'm flying back with you next week when you go home!"

1. Where were the children going?

_____

2. What did they do on the airplane?

_____

3. Where was Aunt Sarah going next week?

_____

4. Why do you think the children had to wear seat belts on the plane?

_____

Write It Right

1. dont do that

_____

2. marys toy octopus has ate arms

_____

3. did alice run in the race on june 6 1999

_____

MATH TIME

Add and subtract.

74	27	37	55	35	27	19	59
+ 17	+ 45	+ 27	+ 28	+ 56	+ 18	+ 26	+ 25

64	97	56	85	93	38	46	56
- 28	- 38	- 17	- 35	- 26	- 19	- 28	- 29

28	50	94	64	19	92	59	36
+ 28	- 37	- 35	+ 29	+ 18	- 15	+ 40	- 17

Monday

©2005 by Evan-Moor Corp. • Daily Summer Activities 2-3 • EMC 1029

Spell It!

Make an X on each misspelled word.
Write it correctly on the line.

1. John hurt his t~~o~~w when he fell.   _____toe_____

2. I gave my mom a pretty red rows.   _____

3. That gote ate my lunch.   _____

4. Dad built a stoan fence.   _____

5. Can you show me how to tie a boe?   _____

Make an X on the misspelled words.

1. noe   no   3. coat   koat

2. slow   slwo   4. flote   float

Copy these words using your best handwriting.

jet plane _____   runway _____

- - - - - - - - - - - - - - -   - - - - - - - - - - - - - - -

_____   _____

airport _____   pilot _____

- - - - - - - - - - - - - - -   - - - - - - - - - - - - - - -

_____   _____

copilot _____   seat belt _____

- - - - - - - - - - - - - - -   - - - - - - - - - - - - - - -

_____   _____

Language Bytes

How many syllables do you hear in these words?

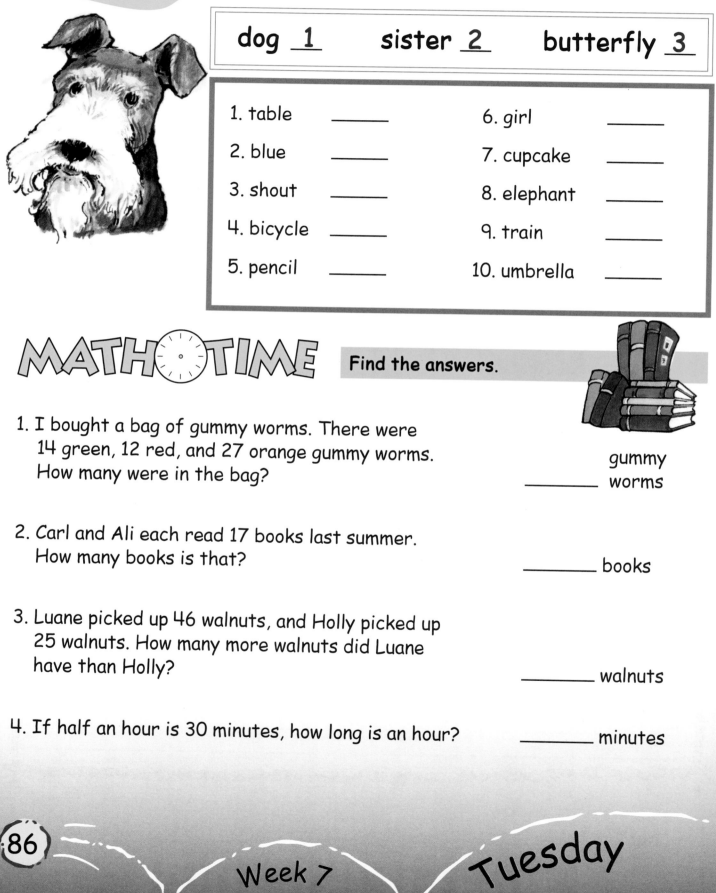

dog _1_	sister _2_	butterfly _3_

1. table _____
2. blue _____
3. shout _____
4. bicycle _____
5. pencil _____

6. girl _____
7. cupcake _____
8. elephant _____
9. train _____
10. umbrella _____

MATH TIME

Find the answers.

1. I bought a bag of gummy worms. There were 14 green, 12 red, and 27 orange gummy worms. How many were in the bag?

_____ gummy worms

2. Carl and Ali each read 17 books last summer. How many books is that?

_____ books

3. Luane picked up 46 walnuts, and Holly picked up 25 walnuts. How many more walnuts did Luane have than Holly?

_____ walnuts

4. If half an hour is 30 minutes, how long is an hour?

_____ minutes

86

Week 7

Tuesday

©2005 by Evan-Moor Corp. • Daily Summer Activities 2-3 • EMC 1029

Do you want to take a trip on a jet plane? First, you must pick a place to go. Then, you buy a ticket from the airline.

On the day you leave, pack your suitcase and go to the airport. You check your suitcase at the ticket counter. It will be put in the cargo hold of the plane. Then you go to the correct gate to board your plane.

When you get on board the plane, find your seat and buckle the seat belt. Listen carefully as the flight attendant gives safety information.

At last, the plane will take off and carry you to your destination. Have a good trip!

Number the sentences in order.

_____ Check in your suitcase.

_____ Go to the boarding gate.

_____ Enjoy your trip.

_____ Listen to the flight attendant.

_____ Go to the airport.

_____ Sit down and buckle your seat belt.

Language Bytes

Match each word with its abbreviation.

1. Mr.	December	5. in.	quart
2. Dr.	Street	6. Sat.	inch
3. St.	Doctor	7. ft.	Saturday
4. Dec.	Mister	8. qt.	foot

MATH TIME

Fill in the missing numbers.

1. 101   102 ___ ___ ___ ___ 107 ___

2. 216 ___ ___ ___ ___ 221 ___ ___

3. 338 ___ ___ ___ ___ ___ ___ 345

4. 450 ___ ___ 453 ___ ___ ___

5. 675 ___ ___ ___ ___ 680 ___ ___

6. 784 ___ ___ ___ ___ ___ ___ 791

7. 896 ___ ___ ___ ___ 901 ___ ___

©2005 by Evan-Moor Corp. • Daily Summer Activities 2-3 • EMC 1029

Ge✦graphy

Use this map to help you answer the questions and follow the directions.

What is south of the doghouse?
Make an X on it.

What is west of the sandbox?
Make a circle around it.

What is east of the flowers?
Color it brown.

What is west of the doghouse?
Color them green and brown.

Write a Story

Tell about a time that you were sick.

_____

_____

_____

_____

_____

_____

Measuring

1. Circle the words that tell how you can measure milk.

gallon   foot   pound

liter   quart   meter

2. Circle the words that tell how you can measure a line.

inch   foot   pound

liter   centimeter   meter

3. Match the question to the measuring tool you would use.

How much do you weigh?   calendar

How fast did the car go?   bathroom scale

What day is it?   speedometer

Language Bytes

Nouns name a person, place, or thing.
Adjectives describe nouns.
Circle the nouns. Make a line under the adjectives.

the <u>rusty</u>, <u>old</u> (bucket)

1. a pretty red dress

2. a round ball

3. two yellow ducklings

4. tall, funny clowns

5. some shiny pennies

6. a cold, wet day

7. an old, dirty shoe

8. noisy little puppies

©2005 by Evan-Moor Corp. • Daily Summer Activities 2-3 • EMC 1029

What is missing?

sun **is to** hot **as** ice **is to** cold

1. **sock** is to **foot** as **mitten** is to _____hand_____

2. **girl** is to **woman** as **boy** is to _____

3. **paw** is to **cat** as **wing** is to _____

4. **in** is to **out** as **up** is to _____

5. **pup** is to **dog** as **tadpole** is to _____

6. **ten** is to **number** as **A** is to _____

7. **sky** is to **blue** as **grass** is to _____

8. **story** is to **read** as **song** is to _____

MATH⏰TIME

Fractions

Write a fraction to tell how much of each picture is shaded.

$\dfrac{1}{2}$ = one piece shaded / two pieces altogether

_____   _____   _____

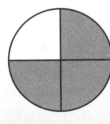 **Friday**    Week 7   91

Unscramble the names of these ways to travel from one place to another.

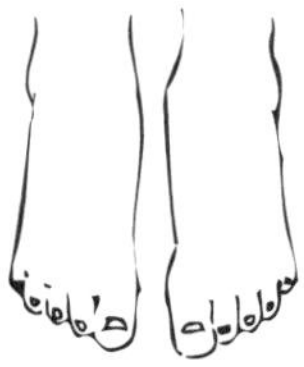

eeft

kruct

pish

sub

elcycib

ratin

plena

rac

toablias

©2005 by Evan-Moor Corp. • Daily Summer Activities 2-3 • EMC 1029

Friday

Color a  for each page finished.

Parent's Initials

Monday   ⭐ ⭐   _____

Tuesday   ⭐ ⭐   _____

Wednesday   ⭐ ⭐   _____

Thursday   ⭐ ⭐   _____

Friday   ⭐ ⭐   _____

Spelling Words

round	frown
house	down
shout	could
about	would
flower	should

What Happened Today? Write about one thing you did each day.

Monday _____

_____

Tuesday _____

_____

Wednesday _____

_____

Thursday _____

_____

Friday _____

_____

Keeping Track Color a book for every 10 minutes you read.

Monday	Tuesday	Wednesday	Thursday	Friday

My favorite book this week was

_____

I liked it because _____

_____

_____

The Contest

Mr. Jenkins put a huge jar of jelly beans in the window of his candy shop. He set a sign next to the jar. The sign read "Win a bicycle! Guess the number of jelly beans in this jar."

Day after day, children in the neighborhood stood in front of the store trying to count the jelly beans. One by one, the children wrote guesses on slips of paper. They put their guesses in the contest box.

On the last day of the contest, a large group of children watched as Mr. Jenkins counted the jelly beans. "There are 856 jelly beans in the jar," said Mr. Jenkins. Next, Mr. Jenkins read the numbers on the slips of paper. "The winner is Tilly Martin," he announced. Tilly rode her new bicycle home, and everyone else went home with a bag of jelly beans.

1. What did the children have to do to win the new bicycle?

   _____

2. How did Mr. Jenkins decide who had won the contest?

   _____

3. Tilly was excited and happy when she won. How do you think the other children felt?

   _____

   _____

   _____

Monday

Week 8

Write It Right

1. will you gimme some of your candy

_____

2. sue and jill doesn't like snakes spiders or snails

_____

3. has mrs guzman done made tacos for dinner

_____

MATH TIME — Multiplication

1	2	3	4	5	5	4	3	2	1
x 0	x 0	x 0	x 0	x 0	x 1	x 1	x 1	x 1	x 1

What happens when you multiply by 0?

_____

What happens when you multiply by 1?

_____

3	5	4	2	5	2	2	4	3	4
x 2	x 2	x 4	x 3	x 3	x 4	x 2	x 3	x 3	x 5

©2005 by Evan-Moor Corp. • Daily Summer Activities 2-3 • EMC 1029

Language Bytes

ow   ou

1. h____se

3. r____nd

5. d____n

2. fr____n

4. ab____t

6. sh____t

Write the spelling words that rhyme with good.

Copy this funny poem using your best handwriting.

I eat my peas with honey.
I've done it all my life.
I know it may sound funny,
But it keeps them on my knife.

_____

- -

_____

- -

_____

- -

_____

- -

_____

- -

Tuesday

Week 8

97

Circle the correct words.

1. Manuel and his sisters _____ on the same team.
   play   plays

2. Her baby _____ crying.
   is   are

3. We _____ making pizza last night.
   was   were

4. Mystery stories _____ exciting.
   is   are

5. A jet _____ over our house every day.
   fly   flies

6. Martha _____ captain of the soccer team.
   was   were

MATH TIME

Find the answers.

1. Jay has 62 baseball cards. Hank has 27 baseball cards.
   How many more cards does Jay have than Hank?   _____ cards

2. Raul ate $\frac{1}{2}$ of the jelly beans. Lana ate $\frac{1}{4}$ of the
   jelly beans. If there were 20 jelly beans,
   how many did they eat?

   Raul ate _____.   Lana ate _____.

3. Billy had 12 pieces of gum. He gave the same
   number of pieces to four of his friends. How
   many pieces of gum did each friend get?   _____ pieces of gum

4. How much is two dozen?   _____

©2005 by Evan-Moor Corp. • Daily Summer Activities 2-3 • EMC 1029

Jelly Beans

It takes a week to make a jelly bean. First water, cornstarch, sugar, and corn syrup are mixed together. Flavorings like cherry or grape are added. The mixture is cooled and poured into tiny molds.

After the centers of the jelly beans harden, they are sprayed with steam and sprinkled with sugar. Then colored syrup is poured over each jelly bean. The syrup dries into a hard shell.

Finally, the shell is polished to make it shine. Seven days have gone by, and the jelly beans are ready to eat at last.

1. Circle what is used to make jelly beans.

corn syrup	cornstarch	water
gelatin	sugar	salt
colored syrup	fruit juice	flavorings

2. Number the steps in order.

_____ spray with steam and sprinkle with sugar

_____ polish the hard shell

_____ mix the ingredients

_____ pour into molds to harden

Wednesday   **Week 8**   99

©2005 by Evan-Moor Corp. • Daily Summer Activities 2-3 • EMC 1029

Language Bytes

Circle the letter for the sound made by the underlined letter or letters.

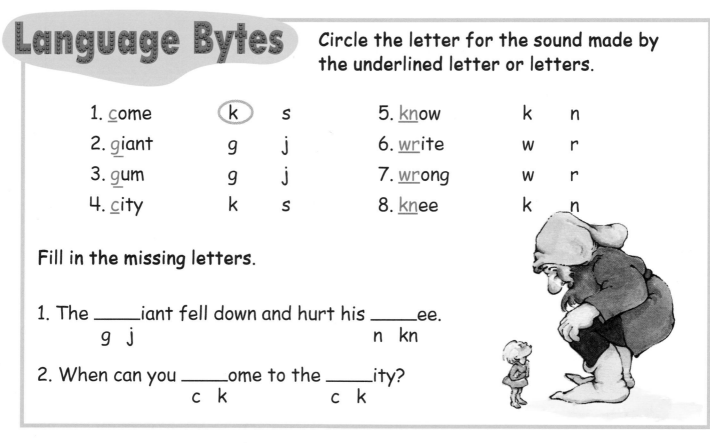

1. <u>c</u>ome   (k)   s
2. <u>g</u>iant   g   j
3. <u>g</u>um   g   j
4. <u>c</u>ity   k   s

5. <u>kn</u>ow   k   n
6. <u>wr</u>ite   w   r
7. <u>wr</u>ong   w   r
8. <u>kn</u>ee   k   n

Fill in the missing letters.

1. The _____iant fell down and hurt his _____ee.
      g   j   n   kn

2. When can you _____ome to the _____ity?
                      c   k   c   k

MATH TIME

Mr. Tosci asked his students, "Do you like pizza, spaghetti, hamburgers, or hot dogs best?" He got these answers:

pizza 卌 l

spaghetti lll

hamburger llll

hot dog ll

Make a graph.

Put this information on the graph.

My Favorite Food

	pizza	spaghetti	hamburger	hot dog
6				
5				
4				
3				
2				
1				

100

Week 8

Wednesday

©2005 by Evan-Moor Corp. • Daily Summer Activities 2-3 • EMC 1029

Geography

A map legend shows symbols for information on the map.

Match these symbols to their water and landforms.

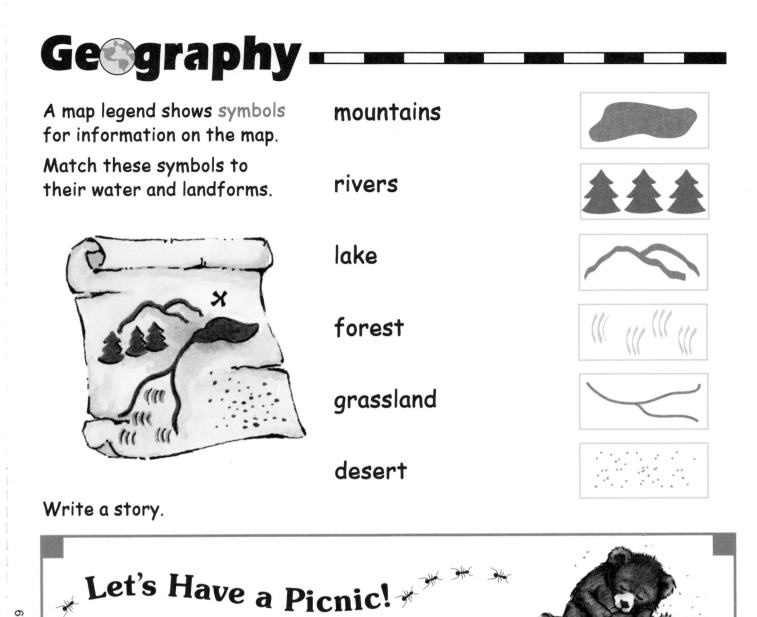

mountains

rivers

lake

forest

grassland

desert

Write a story.

Let's Have a Picnic!

_____

_____

_____

_____

MATH TIME

> = <

1. 7 + 2 (=) 2 + 7

2. 15 - 8 ( ) 12 - 4

3. 14 + 8 ( ) 12 + 10

4. 14 - 6 ( ) 18 - 9

5. 10 + 10 ( ) 15 + 0

6. 3 + 5 + 6 ( ) 10 + 9

7. 5 + 3 + 9 ( ) 14 - 7

8. 5 x 0 ( ) 3 x 2

9. 5 x 2 ( ) 3 x 4

10. 6 x 3 ( ) 4 x 4

Language Bytes

Write the words that mean more than one.

1. hat ___hats___

2. dress _____

3. man _____

4. brush _____

5. fox _____

6. mouse _____

7. box _____

8. tooth _____

9. child _____

10. chair _____

Week 8

Thursday

©2005 by Evan-Moor Corp. • Daily Summer Activities 2-3 • EMC 1029

Language Bytes

Write each word below on the line next to its rhyming word.

lunch	glass	rocks	plate	clay
sky	blew	race	wood	book

1. shook _____

2. class _____

3. place _____

4. shoe _____

5. wait _____

6. fox _____

7. bunch _____

8. sleigh _____

9. high _____

10. could _____

MATH TIME

Circle the answers.

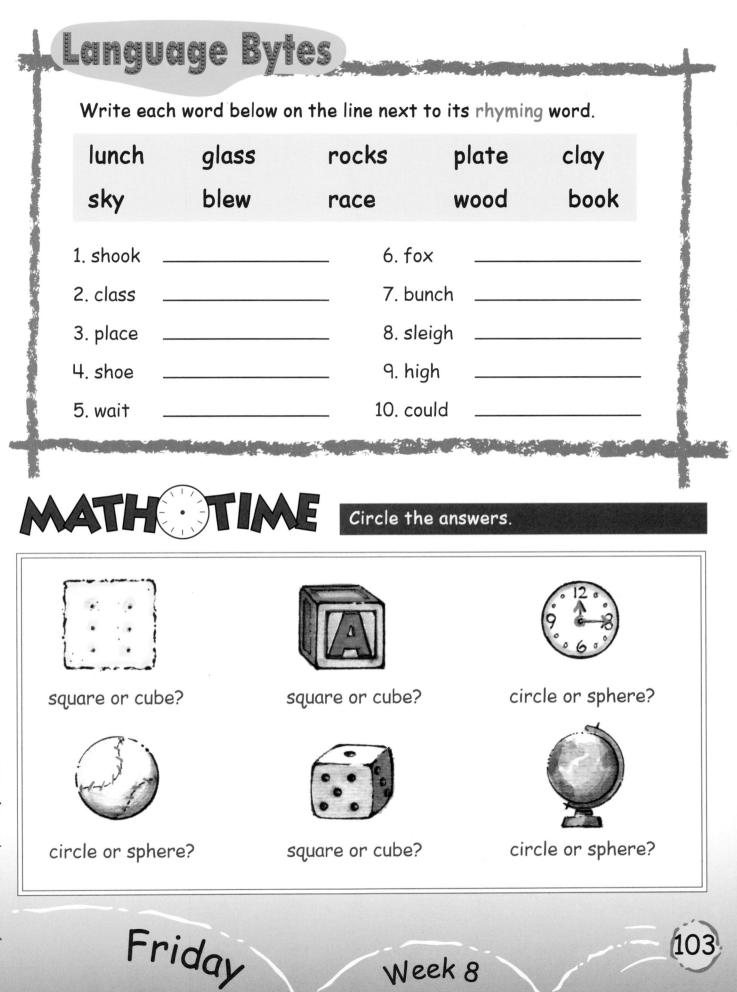

square or cube?

square or cube?

circle or sphere?

circle or sphere?

square or cube?

circle or sphere?

Connect the dots.

1. Start at **A** and connect the capital letters.

2. Start at **a** and connect the lowercase letters.

What did you make?

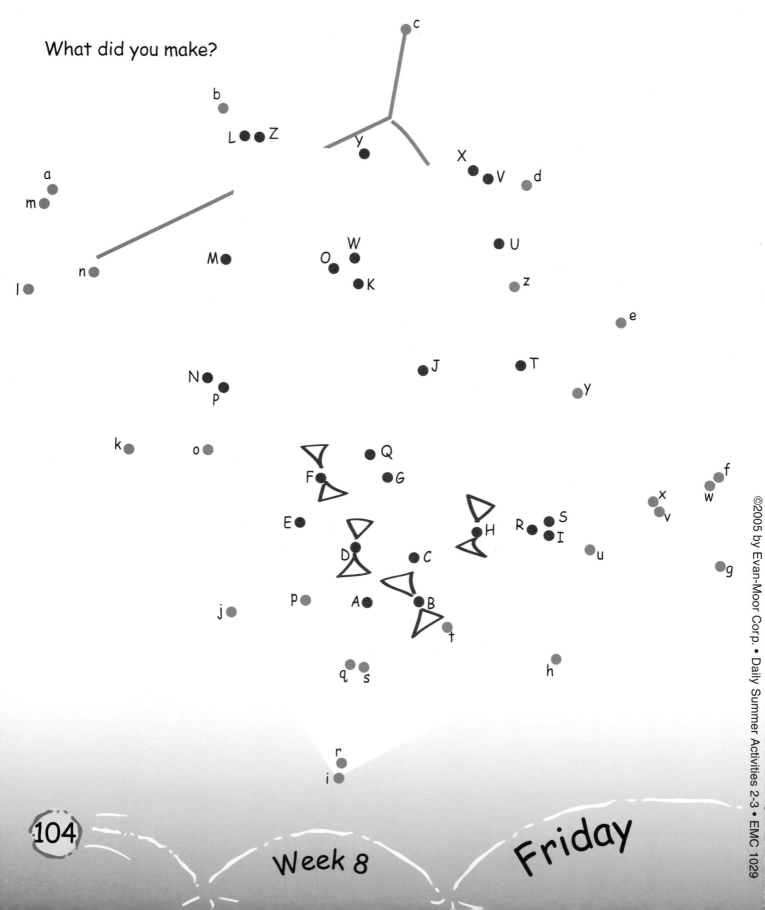

Week 8

Friday

©2005 by Evan-Moor Corp. • Daily Summer Activities 2-3 • EMC 1029

Color a  for each page finished.

Parent's Initials

Monday ☆☆ _____

Tuesday ☆☆ _____

Wednesday ☆☆ _____

Thursday ☆☆ _____

Friday ☆☆ _____

Spelling Words

stopped	skipping
jumped	washing
wanted	throwing
stayed	swimming
helped	saying

Write about one thing you did each day.

Monday _____

_____

Tuesday _____

_____

Wednesday _____

_____

Thursday _____

_____

Friday _____

_____

Keeping Track **Color a book for every 10 minutes you read.**

Monday	Tuesday	Wednesday	Thursday	Friday

My favorite book this week was

_____

I liked it because _____

_____

_____

Arnold's STRANGE Lunch

Arnold's mother was in a hurry to get to work. So Arnold's older brother made his lunch. At lunchtime, Arnold took a big bite out of his sandwich. "Yech!" said Arnold. "My lunch is awful!"

His friends watched as Arnold looked at his sandwich. It was peanut butter and jelly. That was okay, but there was a large sour pickle slice in it, too. Next he took out a whole carrot, green top and all. To make it even worse, there were no cookies. He peeked into his thermos. "Water! He just gave me water!" groaned Arnold.

"Don't worry," said his friends. "We'll share with you." So Arnold had cheese on a cracker, a ball of rice and fish, a tortilla wrapped around beans, a cookie, and half a banana.

"Thanks for sharing," said Arnold. "That was a great lunch!"

1. What was wrong with Arnold's lunch?

_____

_____

2. How did Arnold's friends help him?

_____

_____

3. What is the worst lunch you ever had?

_____

Write It Right

1. why did the babys rattle fell on the floor

   _____

2. theres a sandwich a apple and some milk in my lunch

   _____

3. whats mr lee planting in his garden

   _____

MATH TIME

Add and subtract.

19	18	33	16	34	29	17	17
26	37	22	18	8	35	13	6
+ 23	+ 28	+ 36	+ 25	+ 34	+ 25	+ 15	+ 7

247	183	358	276	950	531	293
- 126	- 70	- 129	- 37	- 628	- 203	- 69

637	383	458	456	750	781	223
+ 126	+ 10	+ 229	+ 37	+ 128	+ 203	+ 69

©2005 by Evan-Moor Corp. • Daily Summer Activities 2-3 • EMC 1029

Spell It!

Add endings to these words to make your spelling words.
For some words, you must double the ending consonant and then add the ending.

ed		ing	
plant	plant**ed**	plant	plant**ing**
pop	pop**ped**	pop	pop**ping**

stop _____

jump _____

want _____

help _____

stay _____

skip _____

say _____

throw _____

swim _____

wash _____

Write a List

Copy this shopping list in your best handwriting.

sour pickles

peanut butter

strawberry jam

bread

bananas

ice cream

_____
- -
_____
_____
- -
_____
_____
- -
_____
_____
- -
_____
_____
- -
_____

Language Bytes

Verbs are action words. Circle the verbs.

swim	dance	build
orange	fly	paint
sing	large	fast
funny	ride	tease
bicycle	laugh	write

Make a list of six verbs that tell **what you like to do.**

_____   _____   _____

_____   _____   _____

MATH TIME

Find the answers.

1. A farmer had 5 goats. Each goat had 4 kids.
   How many kids did he have in all?   _____ kids

2. There are 106 neon fish, 210 goldfish, and 23 catfish
   in the aquarium. How many fish is that?   _____ fish

3. A quart of milk is equal to 4 cups. Ann used 4 quarts
   of milk to make pudding for the party. How many
   cups of milk did she use?   _____ cups

4. Leroy found 2 quarters, 3 dimes, and 17 pennies.
   How much money did he find?   _____¢

©2005 by Evan-Moor Corp. • Daily Summer Activities 2-3 • EMC 1029

Eat Right

Your body is like a car. A car needs fuel to run. Your body needs fuel, too. Food is the fuel your body uses.

The food you eat gives your body what it needs to grow strong and stay well. The food you eat gives your body energy to work and play.

Every day a child under the age of ten should have:

    3 servings or more of fruits and vegetables

    2 or 3 servings of milk and other milk products

    2 servings of meat, fish, or beans

    4 to 6 servings of breads and cereals

If you eat good foods and get plenty of rest and exercise, you will keep growing and have a strong, healthy body.

1. What does your body use for fuel?

_____

2. Why do you need good food and exercise?

_____

3. Name one kind of food in each of these groups.

    fruit _____   vegetable _____

    meat _____   cereal _____

Wednesday

Week 9

Light and fight are part of the same word family.
Add ight to make more words in this word family.

light   s_____   r_____

fight   n_____   t_____

Use the words in these sentences.

1. My old shoes are too _____.

2. My dog got into a _____ with the cat next door.

3. My mom turns on a _____ when it gets dark.

4. Have you ever seen such a funny _____?

5. I caught the ball in my _____ hand.

MATH○TIME

What comes before and after?

_____ 134 _____   _____ 515 _____

_____ 301 _____   _____ 898 _____

_____ 645 _____   _____ 601 _____

_____ 929 _____   _____ 160 _____

_____ 329 _____   _____ 762 _____

_____ 832 _____   _____ 999 _____

©2005 by Evan-Moor Corp. • Daily Summer Activities 2-3 • EMC 1029

Geography

Use this map to follow the directions.

1. Make a circle around the church.

2. Trace the railroad tracks in red.

3. Make an X on the school.

4. Count the houses. _____

5. Count the stores. _____

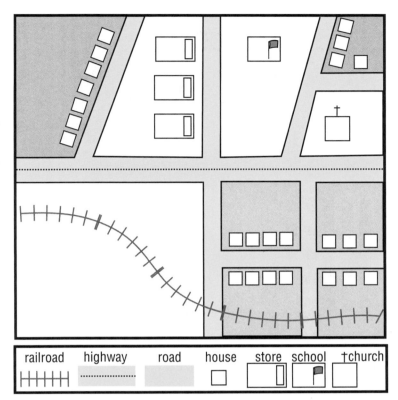

railroad	highway	road	house	store	school	†church

Write a Story

Describe your favorite food. What does it look like? smell like? taste like?

_____

_____

_____

_____

_____

Thursday   Week 9

MATH⊙TIME

How many boxes are in each set?

Key:
- 1 ▪
- 10 (rod)
- 100 (hundred square)

1. _____

2. _____

3. _____

4. _____

5. _____

Language Bytes

Fill in the missing words.

they   them

1. Did _____ want to come to the party?

2. I am going to help _____ paint the fence.

3. _____ will be done at six o'clock.

4. How did _____ build that tall tower?

5. Sam and Pete went with _____ to the beach.

6. Do _____ have to go home already?

©2005 by Evan-Moor Corp. • Daily Summer Activities 2-3 • EMC 1029

Some words change when an ending is added.
Change y to i and add es to these words.

1. lady   _ladies_   5. baby   _____

2. daisy   _____   6. berry   _____

3. pony   _____   7. cherry   _____

4. party   _____   8. body   _____

MATH ⏱ TIME   Draw the shapes.

a shape with no corners	a shape with 5 sides and 5 corners	a shape with 3 corners and 3 sides
a shape with 4 corners and 4 sides that are all the same size	a shape with 8 sides and 8 corners	a shape with 6 corners and 6 sides

Friday   Week 9

Find the fruits and vegetables in this word search.

apple	banana	bean	beet
carrot	celery	cherry	eggplant
fig	kiwi	lettuce	orange
peach	pear	peas	plum
potato	spinach	strawberry	yam

```
c a r r o t b a n a n a o n
h k p e a r e g g p l a n t
e i l a t c e l e r y p o f
r w u l e t t u c e b p r i
r i m o p o t a t o e l a g
y a m p e a c h u p a e n c
s t r a w b e r r y n a g u
s p i n a c h p e a s n e p
```

Now make an X on each fruit in the list.
Make a circle around each vegetable in the list.

©2005 by Evan-Moor Corp. • Daily Summer Activities 2-3 • EMC 1029

Color a ⭐ for each page finished.

Parent's Initials

Monday	☆	☆	_____
Tuesday	☆	☆	_____
Wednesday	☆	☆	_____
Thursday	☆	☆	_____
Friday	☆	☆	_____

Spelling Words

push	because
pull	friend
funny	something
silly	many
happy	who

What Happened Today? Write about one thing you did each day.

Monday _____

_____

Tuesday _____

_____

Wednesday _____

_____

Thursday _____

_____

Friday _____

_____

Keeping Track Color a book for every 10 minutes you read.

Monday	Tuesday	Wednesday	Thursday	Friday

My favorite book this week was

_____

I liked it because _____

_____

_____

Ice Cream

On Sunday afternoons, my family likes to go for rides in the country. On the way home, we stop at a store that sells ice-cream cones. Everybody in my family loves ice cream.

When we visit my grandfather's dairy in the country, we get our ice cream a different way. We make it! Grandfather has an old ice-cream maker. You fill a metal container with milk, sugar, and flavorings and pack ice and salt around the container. Then you turn a handle to move the metal container around. About the time you think your arm is going to fall off because it's so tired, the ice cream is ready. It tastes delicious!

One day when we were visiting some friends, we got our ice cream in another way. A little truck playing music drove slowly down the streets. When it got closer, my friend asked, "Would you like some ice cream?" The man driving the little truck was selling ice cream. Wow! Ice cream delivered right to your house. What a great idea! I don't care where it comes from, I just love ice cream!

1. What does the family in this story do on Sundays?

_____

2. List three ways the people in the story got ice cream.

_____

_____

_____

3. Do you like ice cream? What is your favorite kind?

_____

Write It Right

These words are pronouns. They can take the place of nouns.

she	we	him	me	they
he	it	her	us	them

Change the underlined nouns to pronouns.

1. Bill and Jose are best friends. _____they_____

2. I go to school with Bill and Jose. _____

3. Mrs. Tanaka lives next door to me. _____

4. Can you go to the store for Mrs. Tanaka? _____

5. Kyle is the best artist in our class. _____

6. I asked Kyle to paint my portrait. _____

MATH TIME Find the answers.

1. $1 + 2 + 3 + 4 + 5 + 6 =$ _____

2. $18 - 9 - 3 - 1 - 0 =$ _____

3. $1 \times 1 \times 2 \times 2 \times 5 =$ _____

4. $17 + 3 - 10 + 6 - 8 =$ _____

5. one + four + three - six + eight + zero = _____

6. $24 - 12 - 6 - 3 - 0 =$ _____

©2005 by Evan-Moor Corp. • Daily Summer Activities 2–3 • EMC 1029

Double the final consonant and add an ending.

add ed	**add ing**
mop __mopped__	hit _____
clap _____	drip _____
flap _____	grin _____
slip _____	bat _____
stop _____	clap _____

MATH ⊙ TIME

Find the answers.

1. The party started at 3:00. It ended two and a half hours later. At what time did the party end?

   _____ : _____

2. One day 253 people rode the bus and 106 people rode the train. How many more people rode the bus than the train?

   _____ people

3. It is 563 miles to Yosemite National Park. How far did we travel today if we have 148 miles left to go?

   _____ miles

4. Write a word problem for 23 - 9 = 14.

   _____

   _____

   _____

Tuesday

©2005 by Evan-Moor Corp. • Daily Summer Activities 2-3 • EMC 1029

Spell It! Fill in the missing letter or letters.

| because | friend | push | pull | something |
| silly | funny | many | happy | who |

p_____ll   _____o   some_____ing

funn_____   fr_____nd   pu_____

bec_____se   m_____ny   s_____lly

Write the spelling words that are the opposite of these words.

1. sad _____   4. few _____

2. enemy _____   5. nothing _____

3. serious _____   6. push _____

Copy these tongue twisters using your best handwriting.

Sister Susie sells seashells at the seashore.

_____

_____

_____

_____

Peter Piper picked a peck of pickled peppers.

_____

_____

_____

_____

Try saying each sentence as
fast as you can.

©2005 by Evan-Moor Corp. • Daily Summer Activities 2-3 • EMC 1029

Dairy Foods

When you drink milk, you are eating a dairy food. Dairy foods come from milk. Most of the milk we use comes from cows. Let's see how milk moves from the farm to your table.

A cow is milked in the morning and again in the evening. Some farmers milk their cows by hand, but most dairy farmers use machines to milk the cows. The milk is carried by a tube to a pipeline and then to a cooling tank. The milk must be kept cool so that it won't spoil.

Then the milk is put into a refrigerated tank on a truck and taken to a dairy. There the milk is heated to kill any germs and put into cartons and bottles.

Some milk is made into the other milk products we eat. The next time you eat cheese, butter, yogurt, or ice cream, remember that they all started as milk.

1. Where do dairy products come from?

   _____

2. Why must milk be kept cold?

   _____

3. Name five dairy products.

   _____

   _____

   _____

Language Bytes

The proper names of places start with capital letters. Write capital letters where they are needed.

forest   ^S/sherwood ^F/forest

1. united states
2. swimming pool
3. rocky mountains
4. sunset beach
5. movie theater

6. disneyland
7. lake louise
8. skating rink
9. dallas, texas
10. yosemite national park

MATH TIME

How many wheels do you see?

vehicle	1	2	3	4	5
🚲	2				
🛒	4				
🚲	3				

©2005 by Evan-Moor Corp. • Daily Summer Activities 2–3 • EMC 1029

Geography

Write the correct number on each continent.

1 South America   **2** Asia   **3** Africa   **4** North America

5 Australia   **6** Europe   **7** Antarctica

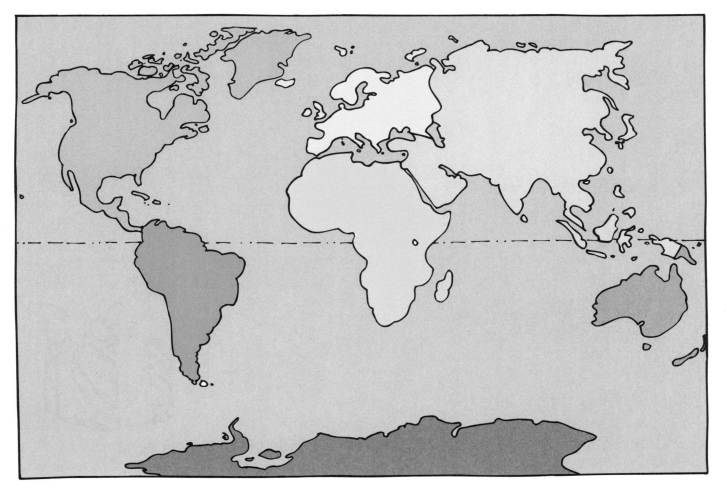

On another sheet of paper, write a story about how to play your favorite game.

How to Play _____

(name of game)

Thursday

Week 10

Draw and continue each pattern.

Example: ABCABC

1. AABCCAABCC

2. ABBCCCABBCCC

3. ABACABACABAC

Circle the naming words (nouns).

1. (James) and Margaret opened presents at their birthday party.

Circle the words that describe (adjectives).

2. A big black hairy spider crawled up the frightened child's dirty leg.

Circle the action words (verbs).

3. When Max heard the phone ring, he picked it up and said, "Hello."

©2005 by Evan-Moor Corp. • Daily Summer Activities 2-3 • EMC 1029

Language Bytes

Correct the mistakes as you copy this letter.

july 1 2000

dear maggie

will you come to my fourth of july party

were gonna play games have fireworks and eat good things

your friend

isaac

_____

_____

_____

_____

_____

_____

MATH TIME

How many coins do you need?

	quarter	dime	nickel	penny
15¢		1	1	
28¢				
35¢				
49¢				

Friday

Pete, Mike, Alice, and Tanisha are in charge of the ball for their teams.
Use the code to find the kind of ball each team needs.

a - 26	e - 22	i - 18	m - 14	q - 10	u - 6	y - 2
b - 25	f - 21	j - 17	n - 13	r - 9	v - 5	z - 1
c - 24	g - 20	k - 16	o - 12	s - 8	w - 4	
d - 23	h - 19	l - 15	p - 11	t - 7	x - 3	

```
  13      30       2      11      36      13       5       7
+ 12     - 4      x 4    + 11    - 11    + 13     x 3     + 8
┌────┐  ┌───┐   ┌───┐   ┌───┐   ┌───┐   ┌───┐   ┌───┐   ┌───┐
│ 25 │  └───┘   └───┘   └───┘   └───┘   └───┘   └───┘   └───┘
└────┘
  b     ____    ____    ____    ____    ____    ____    ____
```

```
  69      16      90       4      77      30       5      50      36       6
- 44    + 10    - 82     x 4    - 55    - 23     x 5    - 24    - 21     + 9
┌───┐   ┌───┐   ┌───┐   ┌───┐   ┌───┐   ┌───┐   ┌───┐   ┌───┐   ┌───┐   ┌───┐
└───┘   └───┘   └───┘   └───┘   └───┘   └───┘   └───┘   └───┘   └───┘   └───┘

____    ____    ____    ____    ____    ____    ____    ____    ____    ____
```

```
   4       3      12      83      14       3
 x 2     x 4    + 12    - 59    + 8     x 3
┌───┐   ┌───┐   ┌───┐   ┌───┐   ┌───┐   ┌───┐
└───┘   └───┘   └───┘   └───┘   └───┘   └───┘

____    ____    ____    ____    ____    ____
```

```
  13       6      28      50      40      18      70       3
+  8     + 6    - 16    - 43    - 15    + 8     - 55     x 5
┌───┐   ┌───┐   ┌───┐   ┌───┐   ┌───┐   ┌───┐   ┌───┐   ┌───┐
└───┘   └───┘   └───┘   └───┘   └───┘   └───┘   └───┘   └───┘

____    ____    ____    ____    ____    ____    ____    ____
```

Friday

©2005 by Evan-Moor Corp. • Daily Summer Activities 2-3 • EMC 1029

Answer Key

Checking your child's work is an important part of learning. It allows you to see what your child knows well and what areas need more practice. It also provides an opportunity for you to help your child understand that making mistakes is a part of learning.

When an error is discovered, ask your child to look carefully at the question or problem. Errors often occur through misreading the problem. Your child can quickly correct these errors.

The answer key pages can be used in several ways:

- Remove the answer pages and give the book to your child. Go over the answers with him or her as each day's work is completed.

- Leave the answer pages in the book and give the practice pages to your child one day at a time.

- Leave the answer pages in the book so your child can check his or her own answers as the pages are completed. It is still important that you review the pages with your child if you use this method.

Page 11

Page 12

Page 13

Page 14

Page 15

Page 16

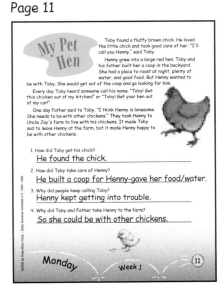

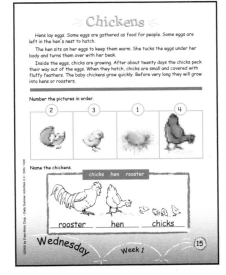

Page 17

Geography

Draw a line from each riddle to the picture that shows the answer.
Write in the name of each picture to complete the sentences.

I am a model of the earth.
I show where land and water
are located. I am round like
the earth.

I am a __globe__

I am a picture of the earth.
I show where land and water
are located. I am flat.

I am a __map__

Write a Story

I would like to have a pet ___Stories will vary.___

Thursday   Week 1   17

Page 18

MATH TIME — Write number sentences.

7, 9, 16
7 + 9 = 16
9 + 7 = 16
16 - 9 = 7
16 - 7 = 9

9, 8, 17
9 + 8 = 17
8 + 9 = 17
17 - 8 = 9
17 - 9 = 8

6, 7, 13
6 + 7 = 13
7 + 6 = 13
13 - 7 = 6
13 - 6 = 7

8, 4, 12
8 + 4 = 12
4 + 8 = 12
12 - 4 = 8
12 - 8 = 4

Write each list in alphabetical order.

ABC abcdefghijklmnopqrstuvwxyz XYZ

orange	1. kiwi
pear	2. orange
kiwi	3. pear

goldfish	1. beagle
parrot	2. goldfish
beagle	3. parrot

book	1. bat
bike	2. bike
bat	3. book

wet	1. warm
warm	2. wet
wool	3. wool

18   Week 1   Thursday

Page 19

Language Bytes — Circle the missing words.

1. Who on the team can run the _____? fast faster (fastest)
2. Sugar is _____ than salt. sweet (sweeter) sweetest
3. Is Mother as _____ as Father? (old) older oldest

MATH TIME — What time is it?

3 o'clock — 3:00
half past 2 — 2:30
5 o'clock — 5:00

6:30 — half past 6 — 6:30
11:00 — 11 o'clock — 11:00
10:30 — half past 10 — 10:30

Friday   Week 1   19

Page 20

Connect the dots. Start at 100.

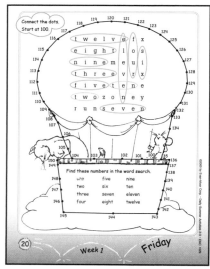

twelve
eight
nine
three
five ten
two one
run seven

Find these numbers in the word search.

one   five   nine
two   six   ten
three   seven   eleven
four   eight   twelve

20   Week 1   Friday

Page 23

Take Out the Garbage

Mother left a note on the refrigerator door. The note said, "Please take out the garbage." This started a big argument. "I took the garbage out last time!" said Mitch.

"No, you didn't. I took it out when you stayed overnight at Pete's house!" shouted Marcus.

"Wait a minute, you two. Fighting won't help," said their older brother when he heard the boys arguing. "Let's do it together. First we have to take out the cans, plastic, and glass and put them in the recycling bins."

As the boys worked, Marcus asked, "What happens to the garbage that isn't recycled?" Jerome explained that the rest of the garbage was taken to the landfill.

"I'll take you there some day so you can see what happens to the stuff we throw away," promised Jerome.

1. Why were the boys arguing?
   __Who must take out the garbage?__

2. What did Jerome suggest that they do?
   __Jerome said to work together.__

3. Where does the garbage that is not recycled go?
   __It was taken to the landfill.__

Monday   Week 2   23

Page 24

Write It Right!

1. mom was make cookies for my lunch.
   __Mom was making cookies for my lunch.__

2. them girls was playing a game.
   __Those/The girls were playing a game.__

3. how many cows was in the farmers barn?
   __How many cows were in the farmer's barn?__

MATH TIME — Name the shapes.

square cone circle
triangle pyramid rectangle
sphere cube hexagon

triangle   cube   square   pyramid

hexagon   cone   rectangle   circle

24   Week 2   Monday

Page 25

Spell It! — Unscramble the letters.

gave use time most
cute find cone she

1. dnif — find
2. ceno — cone
3. vage — gave
4. stom — most
5. meti — time
6. sue — use
7. tuce — cute
8. hes — she

Write sentences using the spelling words that have a long i.

1. Sentences will vary, but must include _time_ and _find_.

2. _____

Use your best handwriting as you write the capital letters.

ABCDEFGHIJKLM
NOPQRSTUVWXYZ

Tuesday   Week 2   25

Page 26

_____ is a compound word.
Underline the compound words in these sentences.

1. My grandmother rides a motorcycle.
2. A butterfly landed on a flower in my backyard.
3. Will you make me pancakes with strawberry jam?
4. Marybeth saw a gopher disappear underground.

Match words to make compound words. Write the new words on the lines.

honey — bee — honeybee
dragon — girl — dragonfly
cow — sauce — cowgirl
apple — fly — applesauce

MATH TIME — Add and subtract.

73 +15 = 88	23 -12 = 11	89 -35 = 54	61 +23 = 84	18 +11 = 29	76 -32 = 44	37 -30 = 7	10 +30 = 40

64 -31 = 33	15 +14 = 29	58 -11 = 47	52 +32 = 84	11 +73 = 84	25 -12 = 13	12 +24 = 36	96 -40 = 56

42 +36 = 78	38 +21 = 59	65 -31 = 34	39 -27 = 12	43 -12 = 31	61 +25 = 86	44 +54 = 98	75 -31 = 44

26   Week 2   Tuesday

Page 27

Where Does the Garbage Go?

Have you ever wondered what happens to your garbage after it is collected?

Garbage is picked up by trucks and taken to landfills away from towns and cities. Landfills are gigantic holes in the ground. The soil is packed hard. Then special liners are put in the holes to keep garbage from seeping into nearby soil.

Garbage trucks dump their loads into the landfill. Workers at the landfill use bulldozers to mash and pile the garbage into level layers. Each day the garbage is covered with a layer of soil.

1. What is a landfill?
   __A big hole where garbage is dumped.__

2. How does the garbage get to the landfill?
   __It is picked up by garbage trucks.__

3. What happens to the garbage after it gets to the landfill?
   __It is piled up and covered with soil.__

4. Think of two ways that you can help make less garbage.
   __Answers will vary.__

Wednesday   Week 2   27

Page 28

Language Bytes — Write each word below on the line next to its rhyming word.

| tie | funny | bed | we | play | fly |

stay	play	pie	tie
red	bed	key	we
sky	fly	honey	funny

Circle the two words that rhyme in each sentence.
1. There were (ten) chickens in the (pen).
2. Uncle Elton spilled apple (pie) on his new (tie).
3. Where did the (nurse) keep her (purse) at the hospital?

MATH TIME — Write the correct sign in each circle.

6 < 9	4 = 4	8 > 2
12 > 9	100 < 101	299 > 199
31 > 13	144 < 414	500 > 300
46 < 64	263 > 236	230 = 230
90 > 60	246 = 246	461 < 473
70 < 77	689 < 890	902 < 920

(28) Week 2 Wednesday

Page 29

Geography

Color the water blue.
Color the land green.

Write a List

Imagine you are about to leave on a trip to a hot place near the ocean. What would you pack for the trip?

Lists will vary.

Thursday Week 2 (29)

Page 30

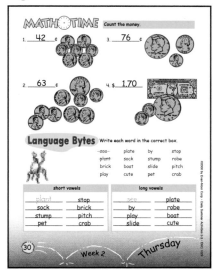

MATH TIME — Count the money.

1. 42 ¢
2. 63 ¢
3. 76 ¢
4. $ 1.70

Language Bytes — Write each word in the correct box.

see	plate	by	stop
plant	sock	stump	robe
brick	boat	slide	pet
play	cute	pitch	crab

short vowels		long vowels	
plant	stop	see	plate
sock	brick	by	robe
stump	pitch	play	boat
pet	crab	slide	cute

(30) Week 2 Thursday

Page 31

Language Bytes — Circle the words that name something (nouns).

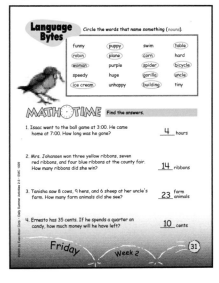

funny	(puppy)	swim	(table)
(robin)	(plane)	(corn)	hard
(woman)	purple	(spider)	(bicycle)
speedy	huge	(gorilla)	(uncle)
(ice cream)	unhappy	(building)	tiny

MATH TIME — Find the answers.

1. Isaac went to the ball game at 3:00. He came home at 7:00. How long was he gone? **4** hours

2. Mrs. Johansen won three yellow ribbons, seven red ribbons, and four blue ribbons at the county fair. How many ribbons did she win? **14** ribbons

3. Tanisha saw 8 cows, 9 hens, and 6 sheep at her uncle's farm. How many farm animals did she see? **23** farm animals

4. Ernesto has 35 cents. If he spends a quarter on candy, how much money will he have left? **10** cents

Friday Week 2 (31)

Page 32

Use the code to solve the riddle.

1 - a	5 - e	9 - i	13 - m	17 - q	21 - u	25 - y
2 - b	6 - f	10 - j	14 - n	18 - r	22 - v	26 - z
3 - c	7 - g	11 - k	15 - o	19 - s	23 - w	
4 - d	8 - h	12 - l	16 - p	20 - t	24 - x	

What is black and white and red all over?

_a_ _p_ _e_ _n_ _g_ _u_ _i_ _n_
1 16 5 14 7 21 9 14

_w_ _i_ _t_ _h_   _a_
23 9 20 8   1

_s_ _u_ _n_ _b_ _u_ _r_ _n_
19 21 14 2 21 18 14

Circle the answer.

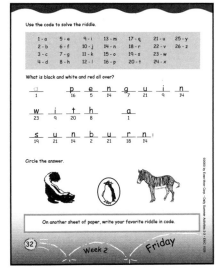

On another sheet of paper, write your favorite riddle in code.

(32) Week 2 Friday

Page 35

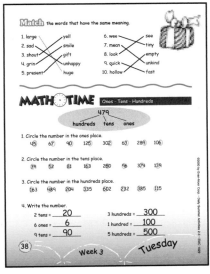

An Elephant Poem

Way down south
where bananas grow
A grasshopper stepped
on an elephant's toe.
The elephant cried
with tears in his eyes,
"Pick on somebody
your own size!"
by Anonymous

1. Where does this poem take place?
   It takes place way down south.

2. Why is the elephant crying?
   The grasshopper stepped on its toe.

3. Do you think a grasshopper could hurt an elephant by stepping on its foot? Why?
   No. It is too small to hurt an elephant.

4. Write something in this poem that could be real and something that is make-believe.
   real: elephants have toes, grasshoppers are real
   make-believe: talking elephants

5. This poem is by Anonymous. What does that mean?
   We don't know who wrote the poem.

Monday Week 3 (35)

Page 36

Write It Right

1. at what time does she party begin
   At what time does her party begin?

2. he gave the toy to kim
   He gave the toy to Kim.

3. dont touch that broken glass
   Don't touch that broken glass!

MATH TIME — Find the answers.

7	6	5	9	6	8	6	9
+ 8	+ 2	+ 8	+ 4	+ 3	+ 5	+ 7	+ 5
24	8	17	14	14	21	22	16

35	44	13	23	30	52	21	24
24	12	22	42	34	15	12	22
+ 10	+ 41	+ 12	+ 21	+ 32	+ 22	+ 34	+ 41
69	97	47	86	96	89	67	87

23	31	22	25	32	63	40	18
43	50	53	42	34	13	12	20
+ 20	+ 17	+ 12	+ 31	+ 32	+ 22	+ 34	+ 61
86	98	87	98	98	98	86	99

(36) Week 3 Monday

Page 37

Language Bytes — Fill in the missing letters.

| th | ch | wh | sh |

| th is | wi sh | sh arp | wa sh |
| ben ch | th en | ch eck | th ank |

Use the spelling words to complete the sentences.

1. I **wish** I had a little bunny **with** a pink nose.
2. That knife is very **sharp**.
3. Dad wrote a **check** to pay for my new shoes.
4. Sit on that **bench** and rest if you are tired.

Copy this poem using your best handwriting.
Gray, wrinkled, saggy, skin
That's the cover an elephant's in.

Tuesday Week 3 (37)

Page 38

Match the words that have the same meaning.

1. large — tiny
2. sad — smile
3. shout — yell
4. grin — unhappy
5. present — gift
6. wee — tiny
7. mean — unkind
8. look — see
9. quick — fast
10. hollow — empty

MATH TIME — Ones - Tens - Hundreds

479
hundreds tens ones

1. Circle the number in the ones place.
   (45) 6(7) 9(0) 12(5) 30(2) 6(3) 28(9) 10(6)

2. Circle the number in the tens place.
   3(9) 5(2) 8(1) 1(6)3 2(8)0 9(6) 3(7)4 1(3)9

3. Circle the number in the hundreds place.
   1(6)3 (4)89 (2)04 (3)35 (6)02 (2)32 (3)85 (1)15

4. Write the number.
   2 tens = **20**   3 hundreds = **300**
   6 ones = **6**   1 hundred = **100**
   9 tens = **90**   5 hundreds = **500**

(38) Week 3 Tuesday

Page 39

An Elephant's Trunk

An elephant's trunk is amazing. The trunk is the elephant's nose. It is used for breathing and smelling, but it has other uses, too.

An elephant eats several hundred pounds of grass, fruit, branches, twigs, and leaves every day. The elephant uses its trunk to gather the food and put it into its mouth. The trunk has a fingerlike tip that helps to pick up food.

The elephant also uses its trunk when it drinks. The elephant sucks water up into its trunk the way you would use a straw. Then the elephant blows the water into its mouth. The elephant uses its trunk to collect water when it takes a bath, too. It sucks up water and then blows it all over its body.

1. List four ways an elephant uses its trunk.

   breathing, smelling, picking up food, collecting water

2. How is an elephant's trunk like your

   nose? The elephant smells with it.

   hands? The elephant picks up things with it.

Wednesday Week 3 (39)

Page 40

Language Bytes
Write the long vowel sound you hear in each word.

1. make _o_ 6. seen _e_ 11. try _i_
2. kite _i_ 7. cute _u_ 12. play _a_
3. she _i_ 8. goat _u_ 13. high _i_
4. use _u_ 9. flea _e_ 14. toe _o_
5. so _o_ 10. pie _i_ 15. eight _a_

MATH TIME — Find the answers.

1. Mr. Stern bought satin ribbons for his daughters. He got 12 each of blue, yellow, green, and red. How many ribbons did he buy? **48** ribbons

2. There were 25 children swimming in the pool. Then 13 got out of the pool. How many were still in the water? **12** children

3. Maria wanted an ice-cream cone with two scoops of ice cream. A scoop of ice cream is 40¢ and a cone is 15¢. How much will it cost in all? **95** ¢

4. What is half of 12? How did you get the answer? **6**

   Answers will vary. (example—"I know that 12 is 6 + 6, so half is 6.")

(40) Week 3 **Wednesday**

Page 41

Geography
Write the four directions in the correct places on this map.

north south east west

north
west east
south

Write N, S, E, and W in the correct places to show north, south, east, and west on this compass rose.

N
W   E
S

Read the chart, then write about elephants.

Elephants
weigh 8 tons
big ears
long trunk
thick, wrinkled skin
tusks

Answers will vary.

Thursday Week 3 (41)

Page 42

MATH TIME — Write the correct ordinal number under each clown.

first second third fourth fifth sixth

fourth	second	sixth
third	fifth	first

Language Bytes
Number the sentences in order to tell a story.

3 Nan paid for their tickets.
2 The children walked up to the ticket counter.
1 Father drove Alex and Nan to the theater.
4 Alex and Nan watched the show.
5 Father came to pick up the children and take them home.

(42) Week 3 **Thursday**

Page 43

Language Bytes
Where does the apostrophe belong?

Barbara's pony   three dogs' bones

1. Tammy's toy kangaroo
2. David's new sneakers
3. Mark's skateboard
4. two rabbits' carrots
5. both girls' dance slippers
6. all the parents' cars
7. both second graders' teacher
8. Amy's two dogs
9. my neighbor's fence
10. a fire fighter's truck

MATH TIME — Count by 2s.

2 4 6 8 10 12 14 16 18 20
22 24 26 28 30 32 34 36 38 40
42 44 46 48 50 52 54 56 58 60
62 64 66 68 70 72 74 76 78 80
82 84 86 88 90 92 94 96 98 100

Friday Week 3 (43)

Page 44

Read the clues to complete the crossword puzzle.

Animals from Africa

Crossword:
3. c h i m p a n z e e
5. z e b r a
7. r h i n o c e r o s
(down: g, b, e, r, a, f, f, e / l, i, o, n / e, l, e, p, h, a, n, t)

Across
3. a large ape with humanlike eyes and ears
5. a horselike animal with black-and-white stripes
7. a large animal with thick skin and two horns on its snout

Down
1. a tall animal with long legs and a very long neck
2. it's not a bird but it can fly
4. a huge animal with big ears and a long trunk
6. a large wildcat

Word Box
bat
chimpanzee
elephant
giraffe
lion
rhinoceros
zebra

(44) Week 3 **Friday**

Page 47

Little Red and the Wolf

A little redheaded girl was skipping along a path through the woods when she met a wolf. The wolf asked the little girl where she was going. Little Red remembered what her mother always said: "Don't talk to strangers." She quickly walked away from the wolf.

Little Red looked around. She saw her friend the woodcutter chopping down a tree. She ran to the woodcutter and told him about the wolf.

The woodcutter chased the wolf away and then walked Little Red to Grandma's house.

Grandma thanked the woodcutter for helping Little Red and invited him to stay for lunch.

1. Where was Little Red going when she met the wolf?

   She was going to Grandma's house.

2. Tell two smart things Little Red did when she met the wolf.

   She walked away fast.
   She found someone to help her.

3. How did Grandma thank the woodcutter for helping Little Red?

   Grandma asked him to stay for lunch.

4. What would you do if a stranger tried to talk to you?

   Answers will vary, but should make sense.

Monday Week 4 (47)

Page 48

Write It Right

1. my uncle send a letter to bob and i
   My uncle sent a letter to Bob and me.

2. does dr cruz work in portland
   Does Dr. Cruz work in Portland?

3. next friday angela is going to the dentist
   Next Friday Angela is going to the dentist.

MATH TIME — Add and subtract

73 + 8 = **81**	40 − 7 = **33**	38 − 8 = **30**	61 + 9 = **70**	44 + 7 = **51**	37 − 6 = **31**	64 + 9 = **73**	34 + 5 = **39**
54 − 25 = **29**	92 − 53 = **39**	47 + 23 = **74**	93 − 23 = **70**	50 + 20 = **69**	50 − 16 = **34**	84 − 20 = **64**	58 − 39 = **19**
84 + 19 = **103**	53 − 18 = **35**	27 − 10 = **17**	72 + 16 = **88**	55 + 25 = **80**	70 − 58 = **12**	50 + 50 = **100**	45 + 36 = **81**

(48) Week 4 **Monday**

Page 49

Spell It!
Write the letters that make the sound of a in each word.

a-e ay ai eigh

1. pl **ay**
2. aw **ake**
3. r **ai** n
4. **eigh** t
5. tod **ay**
6. w **eigh**
7. p **ai** l
8. c **ake**

Write your whole name using your best handwriting.

Now write the names of the people who live in your house.

Tuesday Week 4 (49)

Page 50

Write the correct word.

1. Tom and Rocky ___rode___ their bikes to the park.
   rode   rides
2. Our class ___played___ ball at recess.
   play   played
3. My dog ___chases___ butterflies in the backyard.
   chase   chases
4. Grandpa ___walks___ to the corner store.
   walks   walk
5. The kite ___flew___ up in the sky.
   flew   fly

MATH TIME — Find the answers.

1. The parade started at 2:00. It lasted 2 and a half hours. At what time did the parade end?   ___4:30___

2. Aunt Lois bought a sweater. It cost $34. She gave the clerk $40. How much change did she get back?   ___$ 6___

3. Mrs. Brown baked 28 pies. She sold 18 pies and gave away 5 pies. How many did she have left?   ___5___ pies

4. Last year Kris weighed 38 pounds. This year he weighs 54 pounds. How much weight has he gained?   ___16___ pounds

50   Week 4   Tuesday

Page 51

Safety First

Do your parents have a lot of rules for you to remember? Are they always telling you to buckle your seat belt or not to talk to strangers?

Parents want to be sure their children are safe and healthy. Their rules are a way to remind children about what they should and should not do. How many things in this list are rules in your house? Underline them.

1. Look both ways before you cross the street.
2. Buckle your seat belt when you ride in a car.
3. Wear a safety helmet when you ride your bike.
4. Don't talk to or take gifts from strangers.
5. Wear a life jacket when you are in a boat.

Make a list of the safety rules in your house.

___Answers will vary.___

Wednesday   Week 4   51

Page 52

Language Bytes — Match each word with its opposite.

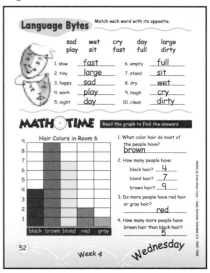

| sad | wet | cry | day | large |
| play | sit | fast | full | dirty |

1. slow ___fast___   6. empty ___full___
2. tiny ___large___   7. stand ___sit___
3. happy ___sad___   8. dry ___wet___
4. work ___play___   9. laugh ___cry___
5. night ___day___   10. clean ___dirty___

MATH TIME — Read the graph to find the answers.

Hair Colors in Room 6

black brown blond red gray

1. What color hair do most of the people have?   ___brown___
2. How many people have:
   black hair? ___4___
   blond hair? ___7___
   brown hair? ___9___
3. Do more people have red hair or gray hair?   ___red___
4. How many more people have brown hair than black hair?   ___5___

52   Week 4   Wednesday

Page 53

Geography

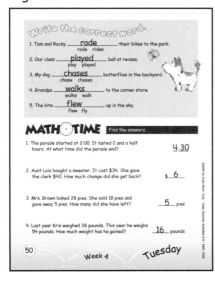

There is an imaginary line around the middle of the earth. It is called the equator. The equator divides the earth in half. Each half is called a hemisphere. Land north of the equator is in the northern hemisphere. Land south of the equator is in the southern hemisphere.

1. Trace the equator in red.
2. Make an X on the hemisphere where you live.

Write a story. Use another sheet of paper if you need more room.

One day as I was walking through the woods, ___Stories will vary.___

Thursday   Week 4   53

Page 54

MATH TIME — Place values

| $20 + 7 = 27$ | $100 + 30 + 2 = 132$ |
| 2 tens + 7 ones = 27 | 1 hundred + 3 tens + 2 ones = 132 |

1. $10 + 8 =$ ___18___
2. $40 + 5 =$ ___45___
3. $60 + 0 =$ ___60___
4. $100 + 90 + 7 =$ ___197___
5. $200 + 20 + 5 =$ ___225___
6. $200 + 8 =$ ___208___

7. 5 tens + 3 ones = ___53___
8. 1 ten + 9 ones = ___19___
9. 8 tens + 5 ones = ___85___
10. 1 hundred + 6 tens + 4 ones = ___164___
11. 2 hundreds + 1 ten + 2 ones = ___212___
12. 3 hundreds + 8 tens = ___380___

Language Bytes

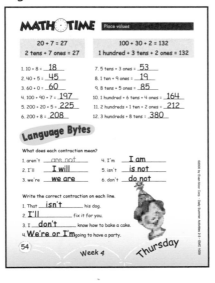

What does each contraction mean?

1. aren't ___are not___   4. I'm ___I am___
2. I'll ___I will___   5. isn't ___is not___
3. we're ___we are___   6. don't ___do not___

Write the correct contraction on each line.

1. That ___isn't___ his dog.
2. ___I'll___ fix it for you.
3. I ___don't___ know how to bake a cake.
4. ___We're or I'm___ going to have a party.

54   Week 4   Thursday

Page 55

Language Bytes — Draw a circle around who or what the sentence is about. Draw a line under what happened.

The (cowboy) rode a horse.

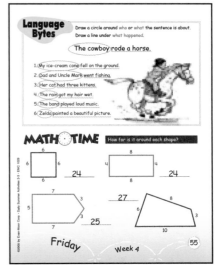

1. My (ice-cream cone) fell on the ground.
2. (Dad and Uncle Mark) went fishing.
3. (Her cat) had three kittens.
4. The (rain) got my hair wet.
5. The (band) played loud music.
6. (Zelda) painted a beautiful picture.

MATH TIME — How far is it around each shape?

___24___   ___24___

___27___

___25___

Friday   Week 4   55

Page 56

Find a path through the woods for Little Red.

Color the boxes as you count by 5s.

			40	15	20
30	40				15
70	50	65	70		65
80					15
		75	80	85	90
	140	110	105	100	95
135	140	145	195	155	
160	175	170	165	130	
	170	115	135	95	105

56   Week 4   Friday

Page 59

A Surprise in the Bathtub

Ginny had been making mud pies in the backyard all afternoon. "You're a mess, kiddo!" said her dad. "It's into the bathtub with you."

"Dad!" screamed Ginny. "Come quick! There's a spider in the bathtub!"

Dad came and took a look. "You don't have to be afraid. It's not a harmful spider."

"I'm not afraid," explained Ginny. "I know it won't hurt me. I don't want it to drown when I turn on the water. Dad helped Ginny gently scoop the spider into a glass. They took the spider to the backyard and let it go. Ginny finally took a bath.

1. Why did her dad tell Ginny she was a mess?
   ___She was dirty.___

2. What did Ginny's dad mean when he said the spider was not harmful?
   ___That means the spider wouldn't hurt anyone.___

3. Why did Ginny want to get the spider out of the bathtub?
   ___She didn't want it to drown.___

Monday   Week 5   59

Page 60

Write It Right

1. were going to canada in july
   ___We're going to Canada in July.___

2. we don't have no sisters
   ___We don't have any sisters.___

3. kelly peter and mike goed to the zoo
   ___Kelly, Peter, and Mike went to the zoo.___

MATH TIME — Multiplication

$2 \times 3 =$ ___6___	$3 \times 4 =$ ___12___	$1 \times 4 =$ ___4___
$2 \times 1 =$ ___2___	$2 \times 2 =$ ___4___	$5 \times 3 =$ ___15___
$4 \times 4 =$ ___16___	$3 \times 1 =$ ___3___	$0 \times 2 =$ ___0___
$4 \times 2 =$ ___8___	$3 \times 0 =$ ___0___	$5 \times 1 =$ ___5___
$3 \times 5 =$ ___15___	$4 \times 3 =$ ___12___	$3 \times 5 =$ ___15___

4	3	1	1	3	2	5
×5	×2	×2	×1	×3	×3	×5
20	6	2	1	10	9	8	25

60   Week 5   Monday

Page 61

Spell It! — Circle the words that are spelled correctly.

1. dera **read**
2. **week** kewe
3. noeb **bean**
4. **sleep** peles
5. **seen** nese
6. celan **clean**
7. twees **sweet**
8. **treat** retat

Write a sentence using the spelling words that rhyme with **meet**.

1. Sentences will vary, but they must contain
2. sweet and treat.

Copy this poem using your best handwriting.

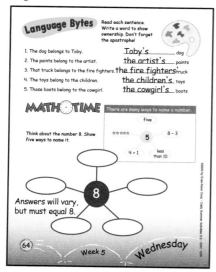

I saw a spider start to spin
A spider web to go hunting in.
She used three pairs of spinnerets
Creating beautiful sticky nets.

Tuesday — Week 5 — (61)

Page 62

CAPITAL LETTERS

The names of people, pets, and places begin with capital letters. Copy the words. Use a capital letter where it is needed.

1. max and amy — Max and Amy
2. my cat ollie — My cat Ollie
3. new york city — New York City
4. mrs. garcia — Mrs. Garcia
5. kim and i — Kim and I

MATH TIME — How long is each animal?

4 inches
3½ inches
6 centimeters
10 centimeters

(62) — Week 5 — Tuesday

Page 63

Spiders
What has eight legs and can spin silk?

Answer: A spider

There are thousands of kinds of spiders. They are different shapes, sizes, and colors. They live in different places. But all spiders are alike in these ways:

Spiders have eight legs.
Spiders have a hard outer skeleton.
Spiders have two main body parts.
Spiders spin silk threads from spinnerets.

Spiders use silk webs to help catch food. Some spiders use silk threads to move through the air from one place to another. Spiders that live underground line their homes with silk. There is even a spider that lives in the water inside a home made of silk.

Spiders may look scary, but only a few kinds are harmful to humans. Most spiders are helpful because they eat insects.

1. How are all spiders the same?
   Answers must give facts from the story.
2. In what ways do spiders use their silk?
   Answers must give facts from the story.
3. How are spiders helpful?
   Spiders help by eating insects.

Wednesday — Week 5 — (63)

Page 64

Language Bytes — Read each sentence. Write a word to show ownership. Don't forget the apostrophe!

1. The dog belongs to Toby. — Toby's dog
2. The paints belong to the artist. — the artist's paints
3. That truck belongs to the fire fighters. — the fire fighters' truck
4. The toys belong to the children. — the children's toys
5. Those boots belong to the cowgirl. — the cowgirl's boots

MATH TIME — There are many ways to name a number.

five
★★★★★ 5 8 - 3
4 + 1 less than 10.

Think about the number 8. Show five ways to name it.

8

Answers will vary, but must equal 8.

(64) — Week 5 — Wednesday

Page 65

Geography

Use this map of North America to help you answer the questions.

1. Which country is north of the United States?
   Canada
2. Which country is south of the United States?
   Mexico
3. Which country has more land— Canada or Mexico?
   Canada
4. Make an X on the Pacific Ocean. Make a ✔ on the Atlantic Ocean.

What do you look like? Look at yourself in a mirror. Think about your hair, your eyes, and your face. Describe yourself.

Descriptions will vary.

Thursday — Week 5 — (65)

Page 66

MATH TIME — Find the answers.

1. Chef Roy baked 4 birthday cakes. He put 8 candles on each cake. How many candles did he use? — 32 candles
2. Jamal spent 85¢ on a muffin and 30¢ on milk. How much did his snack cost? — $1.15
3. If one goat has 4 legs, how many legs will 10 goats have? — 40 legs
4. The farmer gathered 3 dozen eggs. How many did he gather? — 36 eggs

Language Bytes — Underline what the speaker is saying.

Carlos said, "My tooth is loose."

1. "Can you help me wash the car?" asked Tony.
2. Mother said, "We're going to the zoo on Sunday."
3. Annie said, "I like chocolate on my ice cream."
4. "Please buy some of my cookies," said the Girl Scout.
5. Mark shouted, "Don't do that!"
6. "I wish I had a puppy," said Kyle.

(66) — Week 5 — Thursday

Page 67

Spell It! — Write an ending after each letter to make new words. Read the words you made to someone.

old	**g**old	**m**old	**s**old	**f**old
and	**b**and	**h**and	**s**and	**st**and
ill	**b**ill	**f**ill	**p**ill	**sp**ill

Write the missing words.

1. Jack **sold** the cow for a handful of beans.
2. We had to **stand** in line a long time to buy tickets.
3. Try not to **spill** your grape juice on the white rug.

MATH TIME — How many apples?

10 ones = 1 ten

+ = 32
+ = 25
= 50

Friday — Week 5 — (67)

Page 68

Spiders

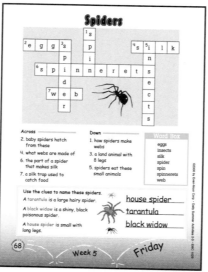

Crossword:
2. e g g s
6. s p i n n e r e t s
7. w e b
(down) s p i d e r, s i l k, i n s e c t s

Across
2. baby spiders hatch from these
4. what webs are made of
6. the part of a spider that makes silk
7. a silk trap used to catch food

Down
1. how spiders make webs
3. a land animal with 8 legs
5. spiders eat these small animals

Word Box
eggs
insects
silk
spider
spin
spinnerets
web

Use the clues to name these spiders.
A tarantula is a large hairy spider. — house spider
A black widow is a shiny, black poisonous spider. — tarantula
A house spider is small with long legs. — black widow

(68) — Week 5 — Friday

Page 71

Margo's Dream

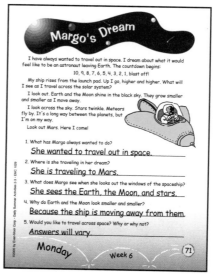

I have always wanted to travel out in space. I dream about what it would feel like to be an astronaut leaving Earth. The countdown begins:

10, 9, 8, 7, 6, 5, 4, 3, 2, 1, blast off!

My ship rises from the launch pad. Up I go, higher and higher. What will I see as I travel across the solar system?

I look out. Earth and the Moon shine in the black sky. They grow smaller and smaller as I move away.

I look across the sky. Stars twinkle. Meteors fly by. It's a long way between the planets, but I'm on my way.

Look out Mars. Here I come!

1. What has Margo always wanted to do?
   She wanted to travel out in space.
2. Where is she traveling in her dream?
   She is traveling to Mars.
3. What does Margo see when she looks out the windows of the spaceship?
   She sees the Earth, the Moon, and stars.
4. Why do Earth and the Moon look smaller and smaller?
   Because the ship is moving away from them.
5. Would you like to travel across space? Why or why not?
   Answers will vary.

Monday — Week 6 — (71)

Page 72

Write It Right

1. there arent no fish in the bowl
   There aren't any fish in the bowl.
2. i want to ride anns bicycle
   I want to ride Ann's bicycle.
3. what are mrs brown planting in her garden
   What is Mrs. Brown planting in her garden?

MATH TIME — Add and subtract.

21 +18 **39**	30 +9 **39**	58 -24 **34**	74 -30 **44**	43 +16 **59**	87 -35 **52**	52 +46 **98**	31 +27 **58**
38 +2 **40**	73 +8 **81**	30 -9 **21**	60 -12 **48**	46 +14 **60**	53 +27 **80**	72 +19 **91**	61 +29 **90**
95 -65 **30**	72 +19 **91**	88 +8 **96**	31 -15 **16**	63 -21 **42**	54 -27 **27**	80 -50 **30**	27 -9 **18**

(72) Week 6 Monday

Page 73

Spell It! — Fill in the missing letters.

er	ir	ur	ar

1. h**ar**
2. t**ur**n
3. h**ur**t
4. w**er**e
5. st**ar**t
6. f**ir**st

Circle the words that are spelled correctly.

1. ar / (are) / wur
2. (her) / hur
3. (letter) / lettar
4. gril / (girl)
5. (hurt) / hert
6. trun / (turn)
7. (were) / wur
8. frist / (first)
9. (start) / sart

Copy this funny sentence to practice writing all the letters of the alphabet. Use your best handwriting.

The quick brown fox jumped over the lazy dog.

What letter is missing in the sentence? **s**

Tuesday Week 6 (73)

Page 74

Language Bytes — a b c d e f g h i j k l m n o p q r s t u v w x y z

Write each list in alphabetical order.

apple	1. **apple**	whale	1. **water**
ostrich	2. **egg**	weather	2. **weather**
uncle	3. **ostrich**	won	3. **whale**
egg	4. **uncle**	water	4. **won**

cow	1. **castle**	harm	1. **harm**
clock	2. **cent**	hug	2. **his**
castle	3. **clock**	house	3. **house**
cent	4. **cow**	his	4. **hug**

MATH TIME — Find the answers.

1. Dad cooked 23 hamburgers for the picnic. If 19 hamburgers were eaten, how many hamburgers were left? **4** hamburgers
2. Mary spent 20¢, Jill spent 25¢, and Ed spent 32¢. How much did they spend altogether? **77** ¢
3. How many hippos are there if 11 are on the riverbank and 7 are in the water? **18** hippos
4. A clown had 17 balloons. He gave 3 red balloons and 6 blue balloons to children. How many did he have left? **8** balloons

(74) Week 6 Tuesday

Page 75

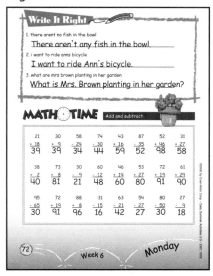

Mars

Mars is one of the nine planets in our solar system. It is the fourth planet from the Sun. It is 141 million miles (227 million kilometers) from the Sun.

Mars is about half the size of Earth. It is a desert except for the ice caps at the North and South Poles. Mars has tall mountains and deep canyons. The soil is full of rust-colored iron dust. This makes Mars look red. Strong winds blow up big storms of red dust.

It is very cold on Mars. This is because Mars doesn't have an atmosphere. There is no air to hold heat from the Sun.

1. How many planets are in our solar system?
   There are nine planets.
2. Why does Mars look red?
   The soil is full of rust-colored iron dust.
3. How much smaller is Mars than Earth?
   Mars is about half the size of Earth.
4. Could you live on Mars? Explain your answer.
   No. There's no atmosphere. It's very cold.

Wednesday Week 6 (75)

Page 76

Write the correct homophones on the lines.

1. My **aunt** lives in New York City.
   A little black **ant** bit my toe. (ant / aunt)
2. A strong wind **blew** the man's hat off.
   Kim has new **blue** shoes. (blew / blue)
3. We **ate** spaghetti for lunch.
   Tony's rabbit had **eight** babies. (eight / ate)
4. Where will you **be** on Saturday?
   A bumble **bee** is fat and fuzzy. (be / bee)

MATH TIME — Color each fraction.

½ brown
½ purple
¼ green
¾ red
¼ yellow
¼ blue
½ red
⅔ blue
⅓ yellow

(76) Week 6 Wednesday

Page 77

Geography

This map shows the seven continents. Draw a circle around the continent on which you live.

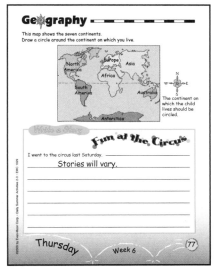

North America, Europe, Asia, Africa, South America, Australia, Antarctica

The continent on which the child lives should be circled.

Write a Story — Fun at the Circus

I went to the circus last Saturday. **Stories will vary.**

Thursday Week 6 (77)

Page 78

MATH TIME — What time is it?

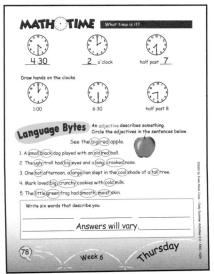

4:30   2 o'clock   half past **7**

Draw hands on the clocks.

1:00   6:30   half past 8

Language Bytes

An adjective describes something. Circle the adjectives in the sentences below.

See the (big) (red) apple.

1. A (small) (black) dog played with an (old) (red) ball.
2. The (ugly) troll had (big) eyes and a (long), (crooked) nose.
3. One (hot) afternoon, a (large) lion slept in the (cool) shade of a (tall) tree.
4. Mark loved (big), (crunchy) cookies with (cold) milk.
5. The (little) (green) frog had (smooth), (moist) skin.

Write six words that describe you. **Answers will vary.**

(78) Week 6 Thursday

Page 79

Language Bytes

Write the words that go together in groups. Give each group a name.

whale	spoon	Mars	fork	jellyfish
shark	Pluto	octopus	star	Jupiter
Moon	knife	plate	tuna	glass

sea animals (group name)	things in space (group name)	things to eat with (group name)
1. **whale**	1. **Moon**	1. **spoon**
2. **shark**	2. **Pluto**	2. **knife**
3. **octopus**	3. **Mars**	3. **plate**
4. **tuna**	4. **star**	4. **fork**
5. **jellyfish**	5. **Jupiter**	5. **glass**

MATH TIME — Draw the shapes.

□ square   △ triangle   ▭ rectangle

How are the shapes alike?
They all have straight sides and corners.
How are the shapes different?
The square and the rectangle have four sides. The triangle has three sides.

Friday Week 6 (79)

Page 80

Connect the dots. Start at 300.

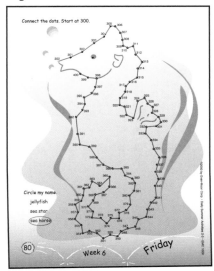

Circle my name.
jellyfish
sea star
sea horse

(80) Week 6 Friday

135

Page 83

Off We Go!

Elton and Beth flew to Memphis for a vacation. When the jet arrived, Aunt Sarah met the children. "How was your trip?" she asked.

"It was awesome!" said Elton. "We've never been on an airplane before. It was huge!

"The flight attendant helped us find our seats and buckle up," said Beth. "It was kind of scary taking off, but then we had fun."

"We got to eat lunch and see a movie. And we took turns looking out the window," said Elton. "Have you ever flown in an airplane, Aunt Sarah?"

"No," answered Aunt Sarah. "But I will. I'm flying back with you next week when you go home!"

1. Where were the children going?
   They're going to Memphis to visit their aunt.

2. What did they do on the airplane?
   Answers will vary, but must reflect the story.

3. Where was Aunt Sarah going next week?
   She was going to fly home with them.

4. Why do you think the children had to wear seat belts on the plane?
   Answers will vary, but should indicate that seat belts are for safety.

Monday • Week 7 • (83)

Page 84

Write It Right

1. dont do that
   Don't do that!

2. marys toy octopus has ate arms
   Mary's toy octopus has eight arms.

3. did alice run in the race on june 6 1999
   Did Alice run in the race on June 6, 1999?

MATH TIME — Add and subtract

74 +17 = 91	27 +45 = 72	37 +27 = 64	55 +28 = 83	35 +56 = 91	27 +18 = 45	19 +26 = 45	59 +25 = 84

64 -28 = 36	97 -38 = 59	56 -17 = 39	85 -35 = 50	93 -26 = 67	38 -19 = 19	46 -28 = 18	56 -29 = 27

28 +28 = 56	50 -37 = 13	94 -35 = 59	64 -29 = 93	19 +18 = 37	92 -15 = 77	59 +40 = 99	36 -17 = 19

(84) • Week 7 • Monday

Page 85

Spell It!
Make an X on each misspelled word. Write it correctly on the line.

1. John hurt his tow when he fell. — **toe**
2. I gave my mom a pretty red rohs. — **rose**
3. That gite ate my lunch. — **goat**
4. Dad built a stoan fence. — **stone**
5. Can you show me how to tie a boe? — **bow**

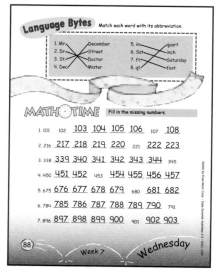

Make an X on the misspelled words.

1. toe ~~no~~ 3. coat ~~kot~~
2. slow ~~slo~~ 4. ~~flot~~ float

Copy these words using your best handwriting.

jet plane	runway
airport	pilot
copilot	seat belt

Tuesday • Week 7 • (85)

Page 86

Language Bytes
How many syllables do you hear in these words?

dog 1	sister 2	butterfly 3

1. table	2	6. girl	1
2. blue	1	7. cupcake	2
3. shout	1	8. elephant	3
4. bicycle	3	9. train	1
5. pencil	2	10. umbrella	3

MATH TIME — Find the answers.

1. I bought a bag of gummy worms. There were 14 green, 12 red, and 27 orange gummy worms. How many were in the bag? — **53** gummy worms

2. Carl and Ali each read 17 books last summer. How many books is that? — **34** books

3. Luane picked up 46 walnuts and Holly picked up 25 walnuts. How many more walnuts did Luane have than Holly? — **21** walnuts

4. If half an hour is 30 minutes, how long is an hour? — **60** minutes

(86) • Week 7 • Tuesday

Page 87

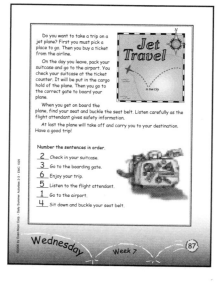

Jet Travel

Do you want to take a trip on a jet plane? First you must pick a place to go. Then you buy a ticket from the airline.

On the day you leave, pack your suitcase and go to the airport. You check your suitcase at the ticket counter. It will be put in the cargo hold of the plane. Then you go to the correct gate to board your plane.

When you get on board the plane, find your seat and buckle the seat belt. Listen carefully as the flight attendant gives safety information.

At last the plane will take off and carry you to your destination. Have a good trip!

Number the sentences in order.

2 Check in your suitcase.
3 Go to the boarding gate.
6 Enjoy your trip.
5 Listen to the flight attendant.
1 Go to the airport.
4 Sit down and buckle your seat belt.

Wednesday • Week 7 • (87)

Page 88

Language Bytes
Match each word with its abbreviation.

1. Mr — Mister
2. Dr — Doctor
3. St — Street
4. Dec — December
5. in. — inch
6. Sat. — Saturday
7. ft. — foot
8. qt. — quart

MATH TIME — Fill in the missing numbers.

1. 101 102 **103 104 105 106** 107 **108**
2. 216 **217 218 219 220** 221 **222 223**
3. 338 **339 340 341 342 343 344** 345
4. 450 **451 452** 453 **454 455 456 457**
5. 675 **676 677 678 679** 680 **681 682**
6. 784 **785 786 787 788 789 790** 791
7. 896 **897 898 899 900** 901 **902 903**

(88) • Week 7 • Wednesday

Page 89

Geography
Use this map to help you answer the questions and follow the directions.

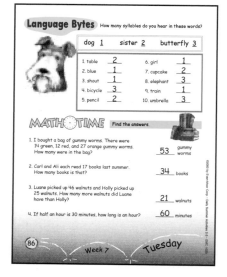

What is south of the doghouse? Make an X on it.

What is west of the sandbox? Make a circle around it.

What is east of the flowers? Color it brown.

What is west of the doghouse? Color them green and brown.

Write a Story
Tell about a time that you were sick.

Stories will vary.

Thursday • Week 7 • (89)

Page 90

MATH TIME — Measuring

1. Circle the words that tell how you can measure milk.
   (gallon) (liter) foot (quart) pound meter

2. Circle the words that tell how you can measure a line.
   (inch) (foot) pound liter (centimeter) (meter)

3. Match the question to the measuring tool you would use.
   How much do you weigh? — calendar
   How fast did the car go? — bathroom scale
   What day is it? — speedometer

Language Bytes
Nouns name a person, place, or thing. Adjectives describe nouns. Circle the nouns. Make a line under the adjectives.

the <u>rusty</u>, <u>old</u> (bucket)

1. a pretty red (dress)
2. a round (ball)
3. two yellow (ducklings)
4. tall, funny (clowns)
5. some shiny (pennies)
6. a cold, wet (day)
7. an old, dirty (shoe)
8. noisy little (puppies)

(90) • Week 7 • Thursday

Page 91

What is missing?
sun **is to** hot **as** ice **is to** cold

1. sock is to foot as mitten is to — **hand**
2. girl is to woman as boy is to — **man**
3. paw is to cat as wing is to — **bird**
4. in is to out as up is to — **down**
5. pup is to dog as tadpole is to — **frog**
6. ten is to number as A is to — **letter**
7. sky is to blue as grass is to — **green**
8. story is to read as song is to — **sing**

MATH TIME — Fractions
Write a fraction to tell how much of each picture is shaded.

$\frac{1}{2}$ = one piece shaded
two pieces altogether

$\frac{3}{4}$ $\frac{1}{6}$ $\frac{4}{6}$

Friday • Week 7 • (91)

Page 92

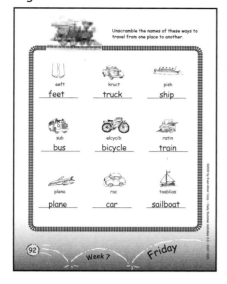

Unscramble the names of these ways to travel from one place to another.

eeft — **feet**	kruct — **truck**	pish — **ship**
sub — **bus**	elcycib — **bicycle**	ratin — **train**
plena — **plane**	rac — **car**	toablias — **sailboat**

Page 95

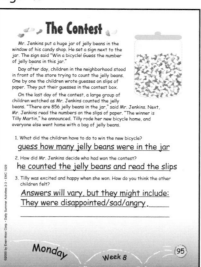

The Contest

Mr. Jenkins put a huge jar of jelly beans in the window of his candy shop. He set a sign next to the jar. The sign said "Win a bicycle! Guess the number of jelly beans in this jar."

Day after day, children in the neighborhood stood in front of the store trying to count the jelly beans. One by one the children wrote guesses on slips of paper. They put their guesses in the contest box.

On the last day of the contest, a large group of children watched as Mr. Jenkins counted the jelly beans. "There are 856 jelly beans in the jar," said Mr. Jenkins. Next, Mr. Jenkins read the numbers on the slips of paper. "The winner is Tilly Martin," he announced. Tilly rode her new bicycle home, and everyone else went home with a bag of jelly beans.

1. What did the children have to do to win the new bicycle?
   guess how many jelly beans were in the jar

2. How did Mr. Jenkins decide who had won the contest?
   he counted the jelly beans and read the slips

3. Tilly was excited and happy when she won. How do you think the other children felt?
   Answers will vary, but they might include: They were disappointed/sad/angry.

Page 96

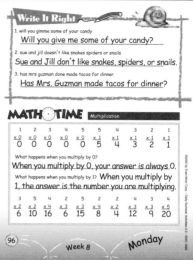

Write It Right

1. will you gimme some of your candy
   Will you give me some of your candy?
2. sue and jill doesn't like snakes spiders or snails
   Sue and Jill don't like snakes, spiders, or snails.
3. has mrs guzman done made tacos for dinner
   Has Mrs. Guzman made tacos for dinner?

MATH TIME — Multiplication

1 ×0	2 ×0	3 ×0	4 ×0	5 ×0	5 ×1	4 ×1	3 ×1	2 ×1	1 ×1
0	**0**	**0**	**0**	**0**	**5**	**4**	**3**	**2**	**1**

What happens when you multiply by 0?
When you multiply by 0, your answer is always 0.

What happens when you multiply by 1? **When you multiply by 1, the answer is the number you are multiplying.**

3 ×2	5 ×2	4 ×4	5 ×3	3 ×3	2 ×4	2 ×2	4 ×3	3 ×3	4 ×5
6	**10**	**16**	**6**	**15**	**8**	**4**	**12**	**9**	**20**

Page 97

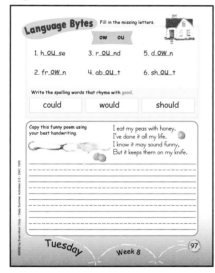

Language Bytes — Fill in the missing letters.

ow   ou

1. h_**ou**_se
2. fr_**ow**_n
3. r_**ou**_nd
4. ab_**ou**_t
5. d_**ow**_n
6. sh_**ou**_t

Write the spelling words that rhyme with good.

could	would	should

Copy this funny poem using your best handwriting.

I eat my peas with honey.
I've done it all my life.
I know it may sound funny,
But it keeps them on my knife.

Page 98

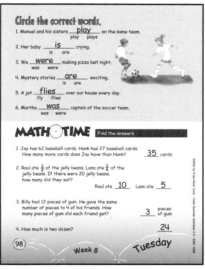

Circle the correct words.

1. Manuel and his sisters **play** on the same team. (play / plays)
2. Her baby **is** crying. (is / are)
3. We **were** making pizza last night. (was / were)
4. Mystery stories **are** exciting. (is / are)
5. A jet **flies** over our house every day. (fly / flies)
6. Martha **was** captain of the soccer team. (was / were)

MATH TIME — Find the answers.

1. Jay has 62 baseball cards. Hank has 27 baseball cards. How many more cards does Jay have than Hank? **35** cards

2. Raul ate ⅖ of the jelly beans. Lana ate ¼ of the jelly beans. If there were 20 jelly beans, how many did they eat?
   Raul ate **10**   Lana ate **5**

3. Billy had 12 pieces of gum. He gave the same number of pieces to 4 of his friends. How many pieces of gum did each friend get? **3** pieces of gum

4. How much is two dozen? **24**

Page 99

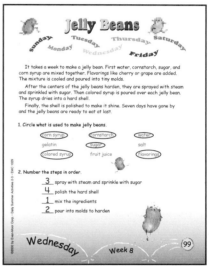

Jelly Beans

sunday   Monday   Tuesday   Wednesday   Thursday   Friday   Saturday

It takes a week to make a jelly bean. First water, cornstarch, sugar, and corn syrup are mixed together. Flavorings like cherry or grape are added. The mixture is cooled and poured into tiny molds.

After the centers of the jelly beans harden, they are sprayed with steam and sprinkled with sugar. Then colored syrup is poured over each jelly bean. The syrup dries into a hard shell.

Finally, the shell is polished to make it shine. Seven days have gone by and the jelly beans are ready to eat at last.

1. Circle what is used to make jelly beans.
   (corn syrup)   (cornstarch)   (water)   gelatin   (sugar)   salt   (colored syrup)   fruit juice   (Flavorings)

2. Number the steps in order.
   3 spray with steam and sprinkle with sugar
   4 polish the hard shell
   1 mix the ingredients
   2 pour into molds to harden

Page 100

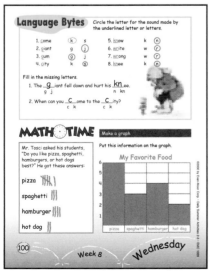

Language Bytes — Circle the letter for the sound made by the underlined letter or letters.

1. come — (k) s
2. giant — g (j)
3. gum — (g) j
4. city — k (s)
5. know — k (n)
6. write — (w) r
7. wrong — (w) r
8. knee — k (n)

Fill in the missing letters.

1. The **g**iant fell down and hurt his **kn**ee. (g/j) (n/kn)
2. When can you **c**ome to the **c**ity? (c/k) (c/k)

MATH TIME — Make a graph

Mr. Tosci asked his students, "Do you like pizza, spaghetti, hamburgers, or hot dogs best?" He got these answers:

pizza — 6
spaghetti — 3
hamburger — 4
hot dog — 2

Put this information on the graph.

My Favorite Food

Page 101

Geography

A map legend shows symbols for information on the map. Match these symbols to their water and landforms.

mountains
rivers
lake
forest
grassland
desert

Write a story.

Let's Have a Picnic!
Stories will vary.

Page 102

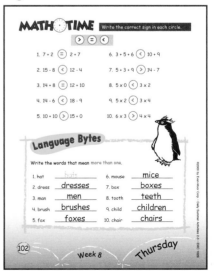

MATH TIME — Write the correct sign in each circle.

> = <

1. 7 + 2 **=** 2 + 7
2. 15 - 8 **<** 12 - 4
3. 14 + 8 **>** 12 + 10
4. 14 - 6 **<** 18 - 9
5. 10 + 10 **>** 15 + 0
6. 3 + 5 + 6 **<** 10 + 9
7. 5 + 3 + 9 **>** 14 - 7
8. 5 × 0 **<** 3 × 2
9. 5 × 2 **<** 3 × 4
10. 6 × 3 **>** 4 × 4

Language Bytes

Write the words that mean more than one.

1. hat — **hats**
2. dress — **dresses**
3. man — **men**
4. brush — **brushes**
5. fox — **foxes**
6. mouse — **mice**
7. box — **boxes**
8. tooth — **teeth**
9. child — **children**
10. chair — **chairs**

Page 103

Language Bytes

Write each word below on the line next to its rhyming word.

lunch	glass	rocks	plate	clay
sky	blew	race	wood	book

1. shook — book
2. class — glass
3. place — race
4. shoe — blew
5. wait — plate
6. fox — rocks
7. bunch — lunch
8. sleigh — clay
9. high — sky
10. could — wood

MATH TIME — Circle the answers.

square or **cube**?
square or **cube**?
circle or **sphere**?
circle or **sphere**?
square or **cube**?
circle or **sphere**?

Friday — Week 8 — 103

Page 104

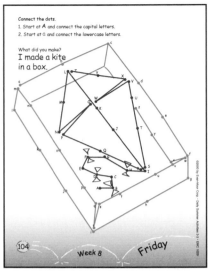

Connect the dots.
1. Start at **A** and connect the capital letters.
2. Start at **a** and connect the lowercase letters.

What did you make?
I made a kite in a box.

104 — Week 8 — Friday

Page 107

Arnold's STRANGE Lunch

Arnold's mother was in a hurry to get to work. So Arnold's older brother made his lunch. At lunchtime Arnold took a big bite out of his sandwich. "Yech!" said Arnold. My lunch is awful!"

His friends watched as Arnold looked at his sandwich. It was peanut butter and jelly. That was okay, but there was a large sour pickle slice in it, too. Next he took out a whole carrot, green top and all. To make it even worse, there were no cookies. He peeked inside his thermos. "Water! He just gave me water!" groaned Arnold.

"Don't worry," said his friends. "We'll share with you." So Arnold had cheese on a cracker, a ball of rice and fish, a tortilla wrapped around beans, a cookie, and half a banana.

"Thanks for sharing," said Arnold. "That was a great lunch!"

1. What was wrong with Arnold's lunch?
His brother gave him foods he didn't like.

2. How did Arnold's friends help him?
They shared their lunches with Arnold.

3. What is the worst lunch you ever had?
Answers will vary.

Monday — Week 9 — 107

Page 108

Write It Right

1. why did the babys rattle fell on the floor
Why did the baby's rattle fall on the floor?

2. theres a sandwich a apple and some milk in my lunch
There's a sandwich, an apple, and some milk in my lunch.

3. whats mr lee planting in his garden
What's Mr. Lee planting in his garden?

MATH TIME — Add and subtract.

19 26 + 23 **68**	18 37 + 28 **83**	33 22 + 36 **91**	16 18 + 25 **59**	34 8 + 34 **76**	29 35 + 25 **89**	17 13 + 15 **45**	17 6 + 7 **30**
247 - 126 **121**	183 - 70 **113**	358 - 129 **229**	276 - 37 **239**	950 - 628 **322**	531 - 203 **328**	293 - 69 **224**	
637 - 126 **763**	383 - 10 **393**	458 + 229 **687**	456 + 37 **493**	750 + 128 **878**	781 + 203 **984**	223 + 69 **292**	

108 — Week 9 — Monday

Page 109

Spell It!

Add endings to these words to make your spelling words. For some words you must double the ending consonant and then add the ending.

ed plant plant**ed** pop pop**ped**	ing plant plant**ing** pop pop**ping**
stop — stopped	skip — skipping
jump — jumped	say — saying
want — wanted	throw — throwing
help — helped	swim — swimming
stay — stayed	wash — washing

Write a List
Copy this shopping list in your best handwriting.

sour pickles
peanut butter
strawberry jam
bread
milk
bananas
ice cream

Tuesday — Week 9 — 109

Page 110

Language Bytes
Verbs are action words. Circle the verbs.

swim	**dance**	**build**
orange	**fly**	**paint**
sing	large	fast
funny	**ride**	**tease**
bicycle	**laugh**	**write**

Make a list of six verbs that tell what you like to do.
Answers will vary.

MATH TIME — Find the answers.

1. A farmer had 5 goats. Each goat had 4 kids. How many kids did he have in all?
20 kids

2. There are 106 neon fish, 210 goldfish, and 23 catfish in the aquarium. How many fish is that?
339 fish

3. A quart of milk is equal to 4 cups. Ann used 4 quarts of milk to make pudding for the party. How many cups of milk did she use?
16 cups

4. Leroy found 2 quarters, 3 dimes, and 17 pennies. How much money did he find?
97 ¢

110 — Week 9 — Tuesday

Page 111

Eat Right

Your body is like a car. A car needs fuel to run. Your body needs fuel, too. Food is the fuel your body uses.

The food you eat gives your body what it needs to grow strong and stay well. The food you eat gives your body energy to work and play.

Every day a child under the age of ten should have:
3 servings or more of fruits and vegetables
2 or 3 servings of milk and other milk products
2 servings of meat, fish, or beans
4 to 6 servings of breads and cereals

If you eat good foods and get plenty of rest and exercise, you will keep growing and have a strong, healthy body.

1. What does your body use for fuel?
Your body uses food for fuel.

2. Why do you need good food and exercise?
So you can grow, and be strong and healthy.

3. Name one kind of food in each of these groups.
fruit _____ vegetables _____
meat _____ cereal _____

Answers will vary, but must be appropriate to the group.

Wednesday — Week 9 — 111

Page 112

Language Bytes
Light and fight are part of the same word family. Add ight to make more words in this word family.

light — **s**ight — **r**ight
fight — **n**ight — **t**ight

Use the words in these sentences.
1. My old shoes are too **tight**.
2. My dog got into a **fight** with the cat next door.
3. My mom turns on a **light** when it gets dark.
4. Have you ever seen such a funny **sight**?
5. I caught the ball in my **right** hand.

MATH TIME — What comes before and after?

133 **134** 135
300 **301** 302
644 **645** 646
928 **929** 930
328 **329** 330
831 **832** 833
514 **515** 516
897 **898** 899
600 **601** 602
159 **160** 161
761 **762** 763
998 **999** 1000

112 — Week 9 — Wednesday

Page 113

Geography

Use this map to follow the directions.
1. Make a circle around the church.
2. Trace the railroad tracks in red.
3. Make an X on the school.
4. Count the houses. **25**
5. Count the stores. **3**

Write a Story
Describe your favorite food. What does it look like? smell like? taste like?
Descriptions will vary.

Thursday — Week 9 — 113

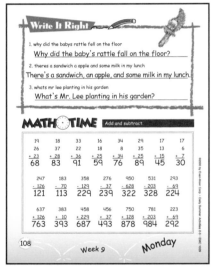

138

Page 114

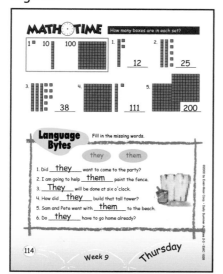

MATH TIME — How many boxes are in each set?

1. 10 100

1.	2.
12	**25**

3.	4.	5.
38	**111**	**200**

Language Bytes — Fill in the missing words.

(they) (them)

1. Did **they** want to come to the party?
2. I am going to help **them** paint the fence.
3. **They** will be done at six o'clock.
4. How did **they** build that tall tower?
5. Sam and Pete went with **them** to the beach.
6. Do **they** have to go home already?

114   Week 9   Thursday

Page 115

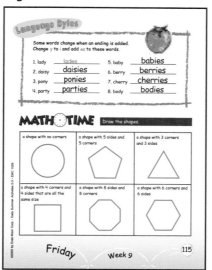

Language Bytes

Some words change when an ending is added.
Change y to i and add es to these words.

1. lady — **ladies**
2. daisy — **daisies**
3. pony — **ponies**
4. party — **parties**
5. baby — **babies**
6. berry — **berries**
7. cherry — **cherries**
8. body — **bodies**

MATH TIME — Draw the shapes.

a shape with no corners	a shape with 5 sides and 5 corners	a shape with 3 corners and 3 sides
(circle)	(pentagon)	(triangle)

a shape with 4 corners and 4 sides that are all the same size	a shape with 8 sides and 8 corners	a shape with 6 sides and 6 corners
(square)	(octagon)	(hexagon)

Friday   Week 9   115

Page 116

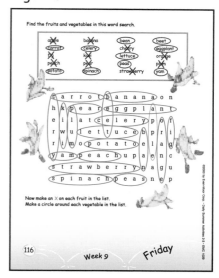

Find the fruits and vegetables in this word search.

apple, banana, bean, beet, carrot, celery, cherry, eggplant, fig, kiwi, lettuce, orange, peach, pea, peas, plum, potato, spinach, strawberry, yam

(word search grid)

Now make an X on each fruit in the list.
Make a circle around each vegetable in the list.

116   Week 9   Friday

Page 119

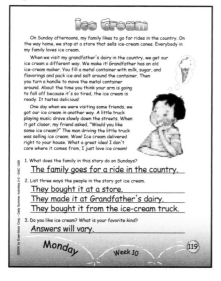

Ice Cream

On Sunday afternoons, my family likes to go for rides in the country. On the way home, we stop at a store that sells ice-cream cones. Everybody in my family loves ice cream.

When we visit my grandfather's dairy in the country, we get our ice cream a different way. We make it! Grandfather has an old ice-cream maker. You fill a metal container with milk, sugar, and flavorings and pack ice and salt around the container. Then you turn a handle to move the metal container around. About the time you think your arm is going to fall off because it's so tired, the ice cream is ready. It tastes delicious!

One day when we were visiting some friends, we got our ice cream in another way. A little truck playing music drove slowly down the streets. When it got closer, my friend asked, "Would you like some ice cream?" The man driving the little truck was selling ice cream. Wow! Ice cream delivered right to your house. What a great idea! I don't care where it comes from, I just love ice cream!

1. What does the family in this story do on Sundays?
The family goes for a ride in the country.

2. List three ways the people in the story got ice cream.
They bought it at a store.
They made it at Grandfather's dairy.
They bought it from the ice-cream truck.

3. Do you like ice cream? What is your favorite kind?
Answers will vary.

Monday   Week 10   119

Page 120

Write It Right!

These words are pronouns. They can take the place of nouns.

she we him me they
he it her us them

Change the underlined nouns to pronouns.

1. Bill and Jose are best friends. — **they**
2. I go to school with Bill and Jose. — **them**
3. Mrs. Tanaka lives next door to me. — **She**
4. Can you go to the store for Mrs. Tanaka? — **her**
5. Kyle is the best artist in our class. — **He**
6. I asked Kyle to paint my portrait. — **him**

MATH TIME — Find the answers.

1. 1 + 2 + 3 + 4 + 5 + 6 = **21**
2. 18 − 9 − 3 − 1 − 0 = **5**
3. 1 × 1 × 2 × 2 × 5 = **20**
4. 17 + 3 − 10 − 6 − 8 = **8**
5. one + four + three − six + eight + zero = **10**
6. 24 − 12 − 6 − 3 − 0 = **3**

120   Week 10   Monday

Page 121

Spell It! — Fill in the missing letter or letters.

because	friend	push	pull	something
silly	funny	many	happy	who

p**u**ll   wh**o**   some**th**ing
funn**y**   fr**ie**nd   pu**ll**
bec**au**se   m**a**ny   s**i**lly

Write the spelling words that are the opposite of these words.

1. sad — **happy**
2. enemy — **friend**
3. serious — **silly**
4. few — **many**
5. nothing — **something**
6. push — **pull**

Copy these tongue twisters using your best handwriting.
Sister Susie sells seashells at the seashore.

Peter Piper picked a peck of pickled peppers.

Try saying each sentence as fast as you can.

Tuesday   Week 10   121

Page 122

Double the final consonant and add an ending.

add ed		add ing	
mop	**mopped**	hit	**hitting**
clap	**clapped**	drip	**dripping**
flap	**flapped**	grin	**grinning**
slip	**slipped**	bat	**batting**
stop	**stopped**	clap	**clapping**

MATH TIME — Find the answers.

1. The party started at 3:00. It ended two and a half hours later. At what time did the party end? **5:30**

2. One day 253 people rode the bus and 106 people rode the train. How many more people rode the bus than the train? **147** people

3. It is 563 miles to Yosemite National Park. How far did we travel today if we have 148 miles left to go? **415** miles

4. Write a word problem for 23 − 9 = 14.
Answers will vary, but must show 23 − 9 = 14.

122   Week 10   Tuesday

Page 123

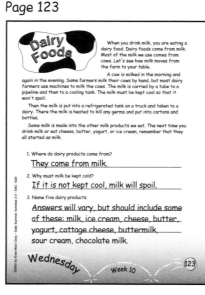

Dairy Foods

When you drink milk, you are eating a dairy food. Dairy foods come from milk. Most of the milk we use comes from cows. Let's see how milk moves from the farm to your table.

A cow is milked in the morning and again in the evening. Some farmers milk their cows by hand, but most dairy farmers use machines to milk the cows. The milk is carried by a tube to a pipeline and then to a cooling tank. The milk must be kept cool so that it won't spoil.

Then the milk is put into a refrigerated tank on a truck and taken to a dairy. There the milk is heated to kill any germs and put into cartons and bottles.

Some milk is made into the other milk products we eat. The next time you drink milk or eat cheese, butter, yogurt, or ice cream, remember that they all started as milk.

1. Where do dairy products come from?
They come from milk.

2. Why must milk be kept cold?
If it is not kept cool, milk will spoil.

3. Name five dairy products.
Answers will vary, but should include some of these: milk, ice cream, cheese, butter, yogurt, cottage cheese, buttermilk, sour cream, chocolate milk.

Wednesday   Week 10   123

Page 124

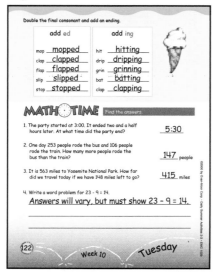

Language Bytes — The proper names of places start with capital letters. Write capital letters where they are needed.

forest — S**herwood** F**orest**

1. **U**nited **S**tates
2. swimming pool
3. **R**ocky **M**ountains
4. **S**unset **B**each
5. movie theater
6. **D**isneyland
7. **L**ake **L**ouise
8. skating rink
9. **D**allas, **T**exas
10. **Y**osemite **N**ational **P**ark

MATH TIME — How many wheels do you see?

vehicle	1	2	3	4	5
(bicycle)	2	4	6	8	10
(wagon)	4	8	12	16	20
(tricycle)	3	6	9	12	15

124   Week 10   Wednesday

Page 125

Geography

Write the correct number on each continent.

1 South America 2 Asia 3 Africa 4 North America
5 Australia 6 Europe 7 Antarctica

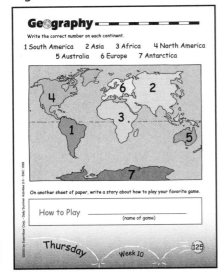

On another sheet of paper, write a story about how to play your favorite game.

How to Play _____
(name of game)

©2000 by Evan-Moor Corp. • Daily Summer Activities 2-3 • EMC 1039

Page 126

MATH TIME — Draw and continue each pattern.

Example: ABCABC ■ ▲ ● ■ ▲ ●

1. AABCCAABCC

Answers will vary, but must follow the indicated pattern.

2. ABBCCCABBCCC

3. ABACABACABAC

Language Bytes

Circle the naming words (nouns).

1. (James) and (Margaret) opened (presents) at their birthday (party).

Circle the words that describe (adjectives).

2. A (big) (black) (hairy) spider crawled up the (frightened) child's (dirty) leg.

Circle the action words (verbs).

3. When Max (heard) the phone (ring) he (picked) it up and (said) "Hello."

©2000 by Evan-Moor Corp. • Daily Summer Activities 2-3 • EMC 1039

Page 127

Language Bytes — Correct the mistakes as you copy this letter.

july 1 2000

dear maggie
will you come to my fourth of july party
were gonna play games have fireworks and eat
good things

your friend
isaac

July 1, 2000

Dear Maggie,

Will you come to my Fourth of July party? We're going to play games, have fireworks, and eat good things.

Your friend,

Isaac

MATH TIME — How many coins do you need?

	🪙	🪙	🪙	🪙	
15¢		1	1		Answers will vary.
28¢	1			3	
35¢	1	1			
49¢	1	2		4	

©2000 by Evan-Moor Corp. • Daily Summer Activities 2-3 • EMC 1039

Page 128

Pete, Mike, Alice, and Tanisha are in charge of the ball for their teams.
Use the code to find the kind of ball each team needs.

a - 26	e - 22	i - 18	m - 14	q - 10	u - 6	y - 2
b - 25	f - 21	j - 17	n - 13	r - 9	v - 5	z - 1
c - 24	g - 20	k - 16	o - 12	s - 8	w - 4	
d - 23	h - 19	l - 15	p - 11	t - 7	x - 3	

```
 13    30     2    11    36    13     5     7
+12    - 4    x4   +11   -11   +13    x3   + 8
 25    26     8    22    25    26    15    15
  b     a     s     e     b     a     l     l

 69    16    90     4    77    30     6    50    36     6
-44   +10   -82    x4   -55   -23    x5   -24   -21   + 9
 25    26     8    16     7    25    26    15    15    15
  b     a     s     k     e     t     b     a     l     l

  4     3    12    83    14     3
 x2    x4   +12   -59   + 8    x3
  8    12    24    24    22     9
  s     o     c     c     e     r

 13     6    28    50    40    18    70     3
+ 8    +6   -16   -43   -15   + 8   -55    x5
 21    12    12     7    25    26    15    15
  f     o     o     t     b     a     l     l
```

©2000 by Evan-Moor Corp. • Daily Summer Activities 2-3 • EMC 1039

Addition Strategies

Plus Zero	Add 0 to a number and the number stays the same. $3 + 0 = 3$
Count Up $+1, +2, +3$	Count up when adding on small numbers, such as 1, 2, 3.
Turn Around	Add numbers in any order and the total stays the same. $3 + 1 = 4$ $\quad$ $1 + 3 = 4$
Doubles	Add the number to itself and that number doubles. $2 + 2 = 4$
Doubles Plus One	Double the number and add one more. $2 + 3 = 2 + 2 + 1$
Tens Partners	There are six sets of number pairs that make 10: $10 + 0$ $\quad$ $9 + 1$ $\quad$ $8 + 2$ $7 + 3$ $\quad$ $6 + 4$ $\quad$ $5 + 5$
Plus Ten	When 10 is added to a number, the tens-place digit increases by one. $12 + 10 = 22$
Plus Nine See 9. Think 10. See 9. Make 10.	To add 9 to a number, add 10 instead and jump back one. See $6 + 9$. Think $6 + 10 - 1$. **OR** To add 9 to a number, make the 9 a 10 by reducing the other addend by one. See $9 + 4$. Make $10 + 3$.

Manuscript Writing

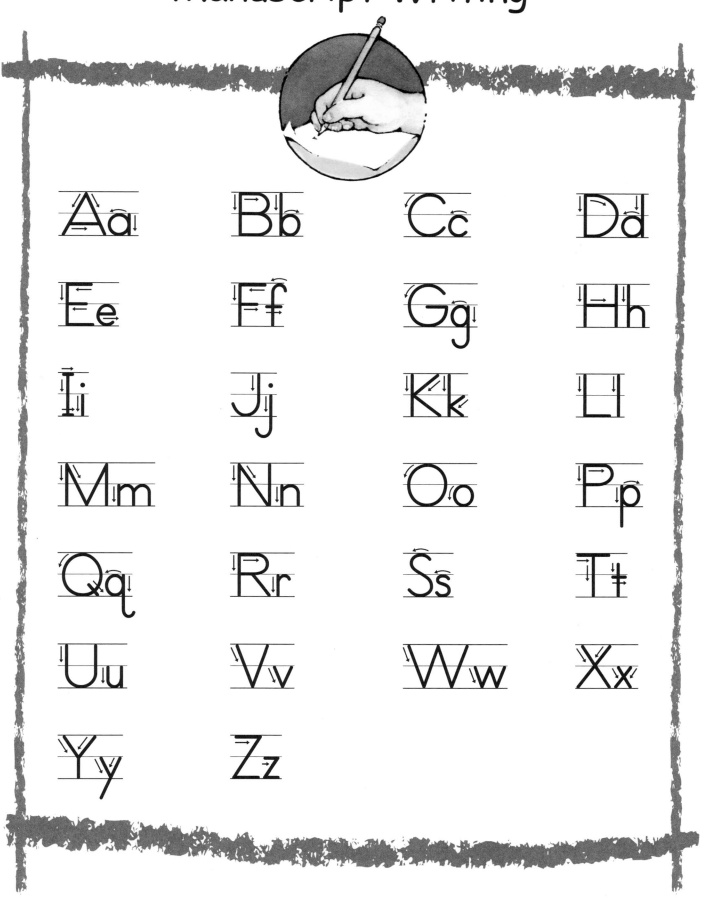